EASY FUN PROJECTS WiTH

Bottle Caps & Lids

**Easy Fun Projects with
Bottle Caps & Lids**
by Kellie Jerman

© 2007 by
Mud Puddle Books, Inc.
54 W. 21st Street
Suite 601
New York, NY 10010
info@mudpuddlebooks.com

ISBN: 978-1-60311-281-9

Printed in China

Table of Contents

People have been storing liquids in bottles for centuries. Of course, with the use of bottles came the need for bottle caps. In the old days, such items as wood and cork were used to keep the liquids in the bottles. However, with the rise of machinery, the metal bottle caps that are commonly used today were invented. These bottle caps are called crown caps, due to the sharp, pointed rim that resembles a queen's crown. However, prevalently used today are plain twist metal and plastic lids.

When making projects out of bottle caps or jar lids, there are several supplies you will need to have on hand.

Bottle caps

The most important supply is, of course, bottle caps! The projects in this chapter use many metal crown caps, as well as the plastic or metal caps. There are many ideas for creating fun and easy projects, but use your imagination! The ways you can craft with bottle caps are practically endless! Use them for animal bodies, eyes, tiddly winks, other game pieces… just about anything.

Adhesives

How do you get your bottle caps or jar lids to stick to the other supplies? Glue, of course! Craft glue is generally called for in these instructions, which is easy-to-use as well as easy to clean up. However, craft glue can sometimes take a bit longer to dry. Feel free to use a cool-temperature glue gun instead of craft glue—as long as you have a responsible grown-up around to supervise! Burning your fingers on heated glue can take all the fun out of your craft projects. So remember to be safe and have your parents, babysitter, or other adult help you when using heated tools.

Double-stick tape is also a great option for making stuff stick. It is also easy-to-use and doesn't make a mess.

Scissors

Everybody knows that scissors are great for cutting. Having a sharp pair of scissors to cut shapes from foam sheets is a good idea, while having a separate pair for paper is ideal. If you cut too many different items with the same pair of scissors, the blades will dull and the scissors won't cut anymore. And what good are scissors that don't cut? Again, if your project calls for some heavy-duty cutting, please ask an adult to help you. It's so much better to be safe than sorry!

Glitter

There's truly nothing better than glitter to glam up a project. But all those sparkly little bits tend to scatter in the wind if you're not careful. Try catching flyaway glitter pieces by folding a sheet of construction paper in half lengthwise, pouring glitter on your project, then using this "glitter catcher" to pour the unused portion back into the container.

Pipe cleaners

Pipe cleaners are so much fun! Fuzzy and bendable, you can embellish your projects with alien antennae, flowers stems, or anything else that can be made from pipe cleaners!

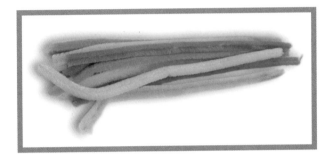

Foam sheets

Foam sheets come in so many colors and shapes. You can even cut your own foam shapes to create anything your brain can think up! Some foam creations are self-adhesive, so you don't even have to bother with glue. Just peel the paper off the back and stick your foam shapes and letters to your projects.
Be wild. Be creative. Have so much fun with foam.

Now that you know a little bit about what you'll be using in the pages ahead, let's get started!

Ugly Guys

What you need:
- Metal caps
- Black permanent marker
- Craft glue
- Cardstock
- Foam: black, red, white, and 3 colors of choice
- Metal paint: black, red, white, and yellow
- Paintbrushes
- Pencil
- Scissors

Instructions

1. Cut 3 Ugly Guys' shapes from cardstock to make your pattern.

2. Trace Ugly Guys' patterns onto brightly-colored foam and cut out.

3. Cut teeth from white foam, mouths from black foam, and tongues from red foam, then glue onto Ugly Guys.

4. Paint bottle caps to desired colors for eyes and let dry.

5. Draw pupils in eyes and any other details you want on your Ugly Guys.

These dolls might be ugly, but they sure are fun to make! Use completed Ugly Guys to decorate your corkboard, or glue magnetic strips to their backs and hang them on the fridge.

Ducks

Try gluing magnets inside these fun little critters for a fancy way to decorate your fridge!

What you need:

- 2 colored plastic caps
- 4 google eyes
- Craft glue
- Feathers
- Orange foam
- Scissors

Instructions

1. Cut beaks from orange foam.
2. Glue google eyes, beaks, and feathers onto bottle caps as shown.

Pigs

What you need:

- Variety of sizes of bottle caps
- Craft glue
- Craft paint: black, pink, and white
- Paintbrushes
- Pink pipe cleaner
- Scissors
- Tiny buttons

Instructions

1. Paint bottle caps and buttons pink and let dry.
2. Glue two bottle caps together for the head and body, then add buttons for snouts.
3. Paint eyes above snouts, then add two dots for nostrils.
4. Cut pipe cleaner to desired lengths and twist into tails and ears. Glue pipe cleaners to pigs.

Caterpillar

What you need:

- 1 metal bottle cap
- 3 colored plastic caps
- Black glitter
- Craft glaze (available at craft stores)
- Craft glue
- Google eyes
- Plastic antennae or pipe cleaner

Instructions

1. Fill metal bottle cap with craft glaze and set google eyes.
2. Add more craft glaze to cap and add glitter. Let set.
3. Glue plastic bottle caps together, then add head.
4. Glue antennae to head.

Note: Get creative when looking for something to add as the antennae. These antennae were found in the bridal section of the craft store.

Ladybugs

What you need:

- Variety of sizes of metal and plastic bottle caps
- Craft paint: black, red, and white
- Paintbrushes

Instructions

1. Paint bottle caps red and let dry.
2. Carefully paint black head, wings, and dots. Let dry.
3. Dot two white eyes on the head and let dry.

Centipede

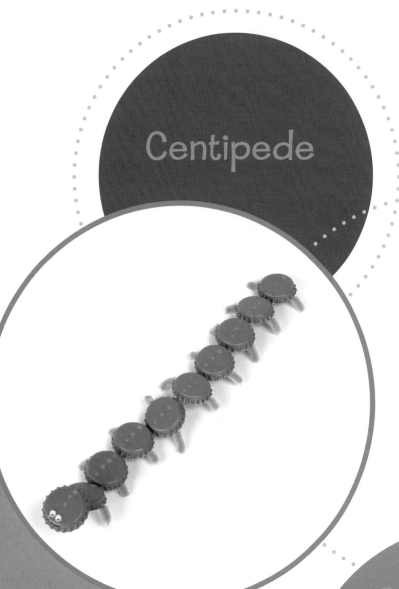

What you need:

- 10 metal bottle caps
- Brown pipe cleaner
- Craft glue
- Craft paint: black, green, and orange
- Google eyes
- Paintbrushes
- Scissors

Instructions

1. Paint metal bottle caps green and let dry.
2. Lay one piece of pipe cleaner down on the tabletop and glue caps to pipe cleaner to create body.
3. Paint orange dots down centipede body.
4. Glue google eyes to head.
5. Cut eighteen 1" (2.5 cm) lengths of pipe cleaner and glue to caps for legs.

What you need:

- 1 large, flat, plastic cap
- 2 metal bottle caps
- Craft glue
- Craft paint: 2 shades green, white
- Foam sheets: 2 shades green, red
- Novelty eyeballs
- Paintbrushes

Frog

Instructions

1. Paint all 3 caps the same shade of green and let dry.

2. Paint spots using second shade of green and let dry.

3. Paint white mouth on front of body and let dry.

4. Cut spots from both tones of green foam and glue to frog body.

5. Cut tongue from red foam and glue to white mouth.

6. Glue novelty eyeballs to the top of the frog body.

7. Glue metal bottle caps underneath the frog body as shown.

Lizard Savings Bank

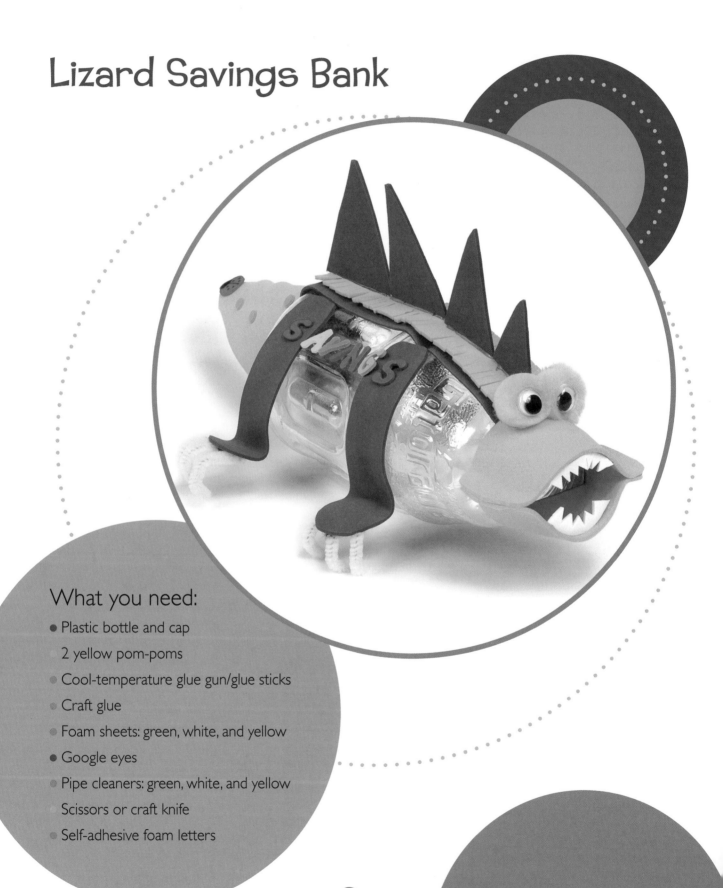

What you need:

- Plastic bottle and cap
- 2 yellow pom-poms
- Cool-temperature glue gun/glue sticks
- Craft glue
- Foam sheets: green, white, and yellow
- Google eyes
- Pipe cleaners: green, white, and yellow
- Scissors or craft knife
- Self-adhesive foam letters

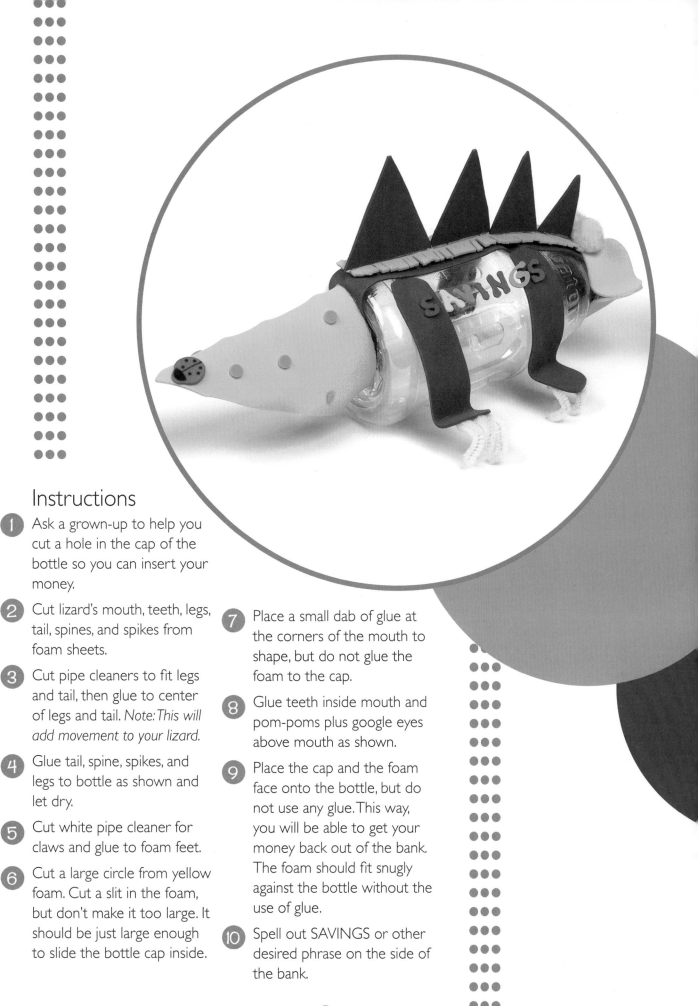

Instructions

1. Ask a grown-up to help you cut a hole in the cap of the bottle so you can insert your money.

2. Cut lizard's mouth, teeth, legs, tail, spines, and spikes from foam sheets.

3. Cut pipe cleaners to fit legs and tail, then glue to center of legs and tail. *Note: This will add movement to your lizard.*

4. Glue tail, spine, spikes, and legs to bottle as shown and let dry.

5. Cut white pipe cleaner for claws and glue to foam feet.

6. Cut a large circle from yellow foam. Cut a slit in the foam, but don't make it too large. It should be just large enough to slide the bottle cap inside.

7. Place a small dab of glue at the corners of the mouth to shape, but do not glue the foam to the cap.

8. Glue teeth inside mouth and pom-poms plus google eyes above mouth as shown.

9. Place the cap and the foam face onto the bottle, but do not use any glue. This way, you will be able to get your money back out of the bank. The foam should fit snugly against the bottle without the use of glue.

10. Spell out SAVINGS or other desired phrase on the side of the bank.

Flower Clown Bank

What you need:

- 5 metal bottle caps
- Glass jar with lid
- Cool-temperature glue gun/ glue sticks
- Foam sheets: blue, green, orange, purple, red, white, and yellow
- Google eyes

  Laundry detergent cap
- Novelty eyelashes
- Pipe cleaners: green, red, and white
- Scissors
- Various sized pom-poms: pink, white, and yellow

Instructions

1. Screw lid onto jar.
2. Glue google eyes, pom-pom nose and pipe cleaner mouth to front of jar.
3. Glue yellow pom-poms onto face around the eyes, nose, and mouth. Glue novelty eyelashes to google eyes.
4. To make skirt, cut foam sheets into squares, then round the corners.
5. Measure and cut hole to match bottle, then slide foam onto bottle in desired order.
6. Cut white foam legs, then glue pipe cleaner to back of legs to give them movement. Add pom-pom feet, then glue legs to base of jar.
7. Make pipe cleaner arms and glue to bottle.
8. Cut foam flowers from desired color and glue to bottle caps. Glue pipe cleaner stems to flowers, then place into laundry detergent lid which will be the flowerpot.
9. Glue flowerpot to top of jar and enjoy!

Purple & Yellow Bird Soda Cozy

What you need:

- 4 metal bottle caps
- Plastic 2-liter soda cap
- 2 google eyes
- 2 purple pipe cleaners
- Craft glue
- Craft paint: green and orange
- Feathers: spotted yellow and yellow
- Orange foam
- Paintbrushes
- Purple foam beverage cozy
- Scissors

Instructions

1. Partially paint the inside of 2 bottle caps green and let dry.

2. Dab glue only at the one edge of each bottle cap and set eyeballs in glue. Hold eyes in place until dry enough to hold. Set aside to dry.

3. Cut a circle from orange foam, then cut a slit in the center of the circle.

4. Place some glue on one side of the foam circle, then push the plastic bottle cap through the glue-covered slit and form mouth. Set aside to dry.

5. Paint remaining bottle caps orange and let dry.

6. Cut feet shapes from orange foam and glue to bottle caps to complete feet.

7. For tail feathers, twist purple pipe cleaners together. Bend up so that you have four lengths of pipe cleaner, then glue yellow feathers to the back.

8. Glue eyes, feet, beak, and spotted feathers to foam cozy.

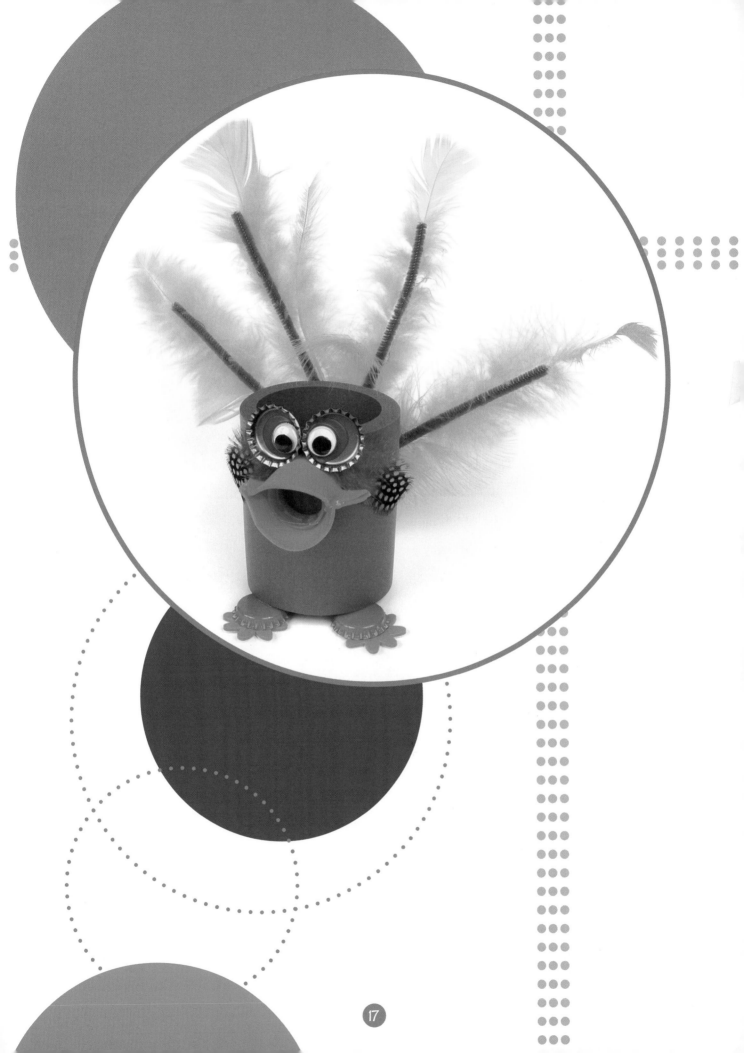

Blue & Yellow Bird Soda Cozy

What you need:

- 2 metal caps
- Plastic 2-liter soda cap
- 2 blue pipe cleaners
- 2 google eyes
- Blue foam
- Blue foam beverage cozy
- Blue paint
- Craft glue
- Feathers: blue and yellow
- Scissors

Instructions

1. Fill metal caps with paint and immediately place the google eyes into the paint. *Note: This will help hold the eyes in place.* Set aside to dry.

2. Cut a circle from blue foam, then cut a slit in the center of the circle.

3. Place some glue on one side of the foam circle, then push the plastic bottle cap through the glue-covered slit and form mouth. Set aside to dry.

4. Cut feet from foam and glue to pipe cleaner legs.

5. Embellish feet with additional feathers, if desired.

6. Glue pipe cleaners to feathers, if desired.

7. Glue eyes and mouth to soda cozy. Let dry.

8. Glue feathers to cozy for wings. Let dry.

9. Enjoy your favorite beverage from your feathery and fun soda cozy!

Orange Sunglasses

What you need:

- 6 metal bottle caps
- Craft glue
- Craft paint: blue, green, and pink
- Foam flowers
- Foam ladybugs
  Orange foam sunglasses
- Paintbrush

Instructions

1. Fill metal caps with different colors of paint and immediately place ladybugs and flowers into the paint. *Note: This will help hold the pieces in place.* Let dry.

2. Glue caps to sunglasses.

Purple Sunglasses

What you need:

- 2 metal bottle caps
- Craft glaze
- Craft glue
- Purple foam sunglasses
- Glitter
- Sequins
- Star-shaped beads

Instructions

1. Fill metal caps with craft glaze and immediately sprinkle sequins and glitter into the glaze.
2. Add star beads, then top off with additional glaze.
3. Let set.
4. Glue caps to sunglasses.

Birds of a Feather Flip-Flops

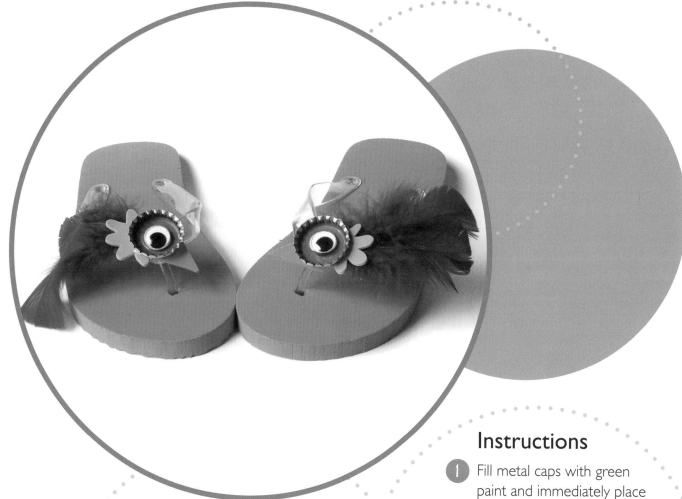

What you need:

- 2 metal bottle caps
- 2 google eyes
- 4 pink feathers
- Craft glue
- Flip-flops
- Foam: light-green and orange
- Green paint
- Scissors

Instructions

1. Fill metal caps with green paint and immediately place the google eyes into the paint. *Note: This will help hold the eyes in place.* Let dry.

2. Cut beak from orange foam and crown feathers from light green foam. Glue underneath bottle cap and let dry.

3. Glue feathers underneath bird head, then adhere to flip-flops.

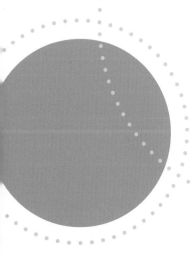

Cupcakes

What you need:

- 3 colored plastic caps
- 3 colors craft paint
- 3 pom-poms
- 3 red beads
- 3 star-shaped beads
- Craft glue
- Glitter: green, orange, and pink
- Paintbrushes

Instructions

1. Glue pom-poms to top of caps.
2. Pour paint over pom-poms, letting it run down the sides of the pom-poms like icing.
3. Sprinkle glitter over wet paint.
4. Glue beads as desired for decorations.

Note: Make sure to cover your work area with newspaper or a plastic tablecloth to avoid getting paint on the table.

Cherry Necklace

Instructions

1 Paint bottle caps red, then sprinkle with glitter while paint is still wet.

2 String beads onto stretch elastic leaving a space between the end of the elastic and the beginning of the strung beads. Tie a knot in both ends of the elastic where beads end and apply a small amount of craft glue to hold the knots secure.

3 Glue one bottle cap to each end of necklace.

4 Place one end of elastic between 2 caps and glue together.

5 To wear your necklace lariat style, cross cherries and flip one through the opening.

What you need:

- 4 metal bottle caps
- Beads: green and red
- Craft glue
- Paintbrush
- Red craft paint
- Red glitter
- Stretch jewelry elastic

Strawberry Necklace

What you need:

- 2 plastic bottle caps
- Craft glue
- Craft paint: black and red
- Green flower tape (can be purchased at your local craft store)
- Green ribbon
- Paintbrushes

Instructions

1 Glue both ribbon ends between bottle caps. Make sure to press tightly until the glue sets so that the ribbon ends remain between the bottle caps.

2 Paint bottle caps red and let dry.

3 Paint black seed spots onto bottle cap strawberries and let dry.

4 Tear 1" (2.5 cm) strips of green flower tape and glue to the tops of strawberries for leaves. Make sure you tear these so they look like real leaves!

Hair Clip

What you need:

- 2 metal bottle caps
- 2 feathers
- Craft glaze
- Craft glue
- Glitter
- Metal hair clip
- Sequins

Instructions

1. Glue feathers to center of clip and let dry.
2. Mix sequins and glitter together.
3. Fill metal caps with craft glaze and fill with glitter and sequins mixture. Let glaze set.
4. Glue caps to center of feathered clip.

Charm Bracelet

What you need:

- Metal bottle cap
- Awl
- Beads: pink and yellow
- Charm
- Craft glaze
- Craft paint: pink and yellow
- Glitter
- Paintbrushes
- Stretch jewelry elastic

Instructions

1. Ask a grown-up to help you poke a small hole in the top of your metal cap with an awl or other sharp tool.
2. Paint back of metal cap pink with yellow polka-dots. Let dry.
3. Fill metal cap with craft glaze, then add glitter and charm. Let glaze set.
4. Thread elastic through this hole.
5. String elastic with beads.
6. Tie ends of beaded bracelet together.

Candle Holders

This is a quick and easy project for creating fun gifts for anyone on your list!

What you need:

- 2 large plastic lids
- 2 candles
- Craft paint: black, red, and white
- Paintbrushes

Instructions

1. Paint lids black and red. Let dry.
2. Paint polka-dots as desired. Let dry.
3. Set candles in lids.

Alphabet Fridge Magnets

What you need:

- 26 metal caps
- Craft glue
- Magnet strips
- Paintbrush
- Scissors
- Self-adhesive foam alphabet
- Yellow paint

Instructions

1. Paint all metal bottle caps yellow and let dry.
2. Stick letters to bottle caps.
3. Cut magnet strips into 26 pieces and glue to the back of metal caps.

Note: Try making number magnets for math problems, teaching a younger sibling to count, or just for fun!

These fun magnets are a great way to learn the alphabet, and if you make multiple letters you can practice spelling words, or leave messages for your family!

Caps Game

What you need:

- 34 metal bottle caps
- Craft glue
- Craft paint: red, white, and yellow
- Glass jar with lid
- Green foam
- Paintbrush
- Self-adhesive foam letters to spell CAPS

Instructions

1. Paint 4 metal bottle caps white and let dry.
2. Add letters to bottle caps.
3. Glue green foam to jar.
4. Stick the word CAPS to green foam.
5. Paint lid of jar red. Let dry.
6. Paint both sides of remaining caps yellow. Let dry.

How to Play:

- Divide the caps evenly between players.
- Place the jar several feet in front of players.
- Take turns tossing the caps into the jar one by one.
- The first player to get a cap into the jar wins all the caps that previously missed the jar. If by chance both players make their first caps into the jar, play continues until someone misses the jar.
- The player with the most caps wins.

What you need:

- 12 metal bottle caps
- 6 self-adhesive foam O's
- 6 self-adhesive foam X's
- 12" (30.5 cm) square sheet of cardboard
- Black permanent marker
- Craft glue
- Craft paint: yellow and red
- Foam flowers and ladybugs
- Paintbrushes
- Ruler

Tic-Tac-Toe

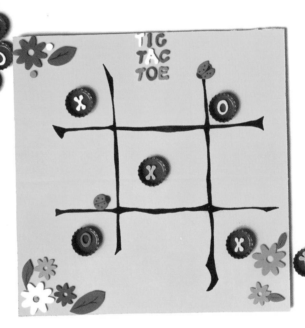

Instructions

1. Paint the cardboard yellow. This will take several coats of paint, and you should let the board dry between each new coat.

2. Draw 2 horizontal and 2 vertical lines as shown.

3. Glue flowers and ladybugs to board corners for decoration.

4. Paint metal caps red on both sides and let dry.

5. Stick X's and O's to caps.

Have fun playing tic-tac-toe with everyone you know!

Checkers

What you need:

- 24 metal bottle caps
- 12" (30.5 cm) square sheet of cardboard
- Black permanent marker
- Craft paint: black, red, and yellow
- Paintbrushes
- Ruler

Instructions

1. Paint the cardboard yellow. This will take several coats of paint, and you should let the board dry between each new coat.

2. Draw horizontal and vertical lines with black marker on the board by measuring 1½" (3.8 cm) at a time.

3. Paint every other square black as shown. Let dry.

4. Paint 12 metal bottle caps red and the remaining 12 bottle caps black.

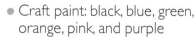

What you need:

- 12 metal bottle caps
- 2 google eyes
- 2 orange foam flowers
- 2 pennies
- 2 red foam ladybugs
- 2 star-shaped beads
- Craft Glaze

- Craft paint: black, blue, green, orange, pink, and purple
- Glitter
- Paintbrushes
- Sequins

Instructions

1. Paint the back of all bottle caps black and let dry.

2. Mix glitter and sequins together and set aside.

3. Making sure to make 2 of each type of bottle cap, paint the insides of the caps any color and fill with star-shaped beads, flowers, pennies, sequins-and-glitter mixture, google eyes, and ladybugs. Let dry.

4. Coat all bottle caps with craft glaze to hold everything together.

Note: These are just ideas to fill your caps with. However, you can be as creative as you like, filling your caps with as many neat ideas as you can come up with to create your match game.

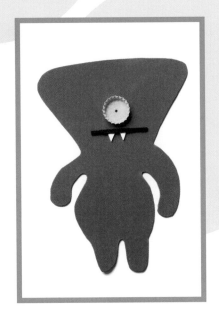

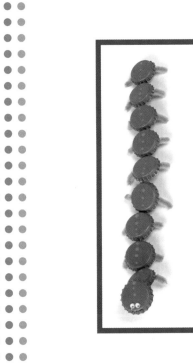

Glitter
Greeting Cards

by Jo Packham

Mud Puddle Books
NEW YORK

Table of Contents

Introduction

Glitz, Glam, and Bling… What are they?

Glitz: flashy, gaudy, showy to the point of being ostentatious.

Glam: razzle-dazzle, sparkle, pizzazz, desirability, pretty, magic, delightful, alluring, charming, romantic, exciting.

Bling: hip-hop term for expensive jewelry and other pricy, attention-getting accoutrements.

Glitter is all that we love and is great fun to use. It adds that extra ordinary, over-the-top touch, and makes everything look fabulous. It will soon be your favorite thing to do!

You are about to enter a designer's world of glitter, glitz, glam, and just plain fun. After a project or two, absolutely everything will look just too plain and pedestrian if there isn't any sparkle.

Welcome to the world of glitter!

Glitz, glam, and bling are all the definition of glitter: glistening, glamorous, brilliant, and showy.

Glitter Greeting Cards
by Jo Packham

© 2007 by Mud Puddle Books, Inc.

Published by
Mud Puddle Books, Inc.
54 W. 21st Street
Suite 601
New York, NY 10010
info@mudpuddlebooks.com

ISBN: 978-1-60311-048-8

Printed in China.

All About Glitter

Glitter is a great way to add flash and flair to cards, gifts and everything. There are a variety of glitters to choose from.

Glitter glue: This type of glitter comes in a tube and is good for writing or drawing finer lines. It does not completely cover large surfaces. As glitter glue is "wet," using too much will cause your paper to wrinkle.

Coarse glitter: The larger bits of coarse glitter are much easier to see than fine glitter. Coarse glitter does not stick to glue very well, and does not provide as much coverage as fine glitter. It can be used by itself or mixed with fine glitter for better coverage.

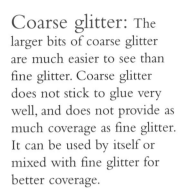

Glass glitter: The oldest form of glitter, glass glitter is actually made from glass. It is available in both coarse and fine, and will tarnish after application.

Fine glitter: The individual pieces of very fine glitter cannot be seen after the glitter has been applied. This is the best type of glitter for card making. It adheres well to the glue and covers completely.

Designer Secrets for Glitter

While working with glitter is fun, remember that it goes everywhere! A small amount of preparation and care will help you prevent finding glitter everywhere forever. Here are a few tips for keeping those shiny bits contained!

* Wear old clothes when working with glitter.

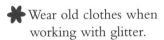

* Pick a work surface that can be easily cleaned. Cover it with brown kraft or scratch paper. Do not use newspaper. The black print will rub off onto your cards.

* Have a "Glitter Getter" and a sheet of plain paper available for each color glitter. When glittering a project, a great deal of glitter is poured onto the project but only a small amount actually adheres to glue. A Glitter Getter will help you pour leftover glitter back into container. This way, a small container of glitter will last for many many projects. To make a Glitter Getter, see instructions on page 21.

* When you are finished using one color glitter, pour excess back into container immediately and replace lid. This will prevent glitter from spilling or spreading everywhere when not in use.

* When finished glittering, wash your hands with soap and water.

WHITE   COPPER

ROSE   GREEN

COMBINATION COLOR   COMBINATION COLOR

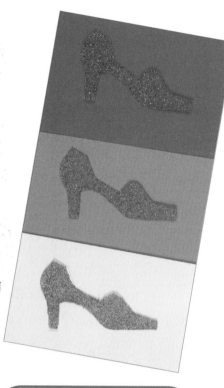

Designer Technique: Shading with Glitter

1. Try "shading" by simply using two or more colors of glitter.

2. Lightly sprinkle the first color onto the glue or adhesive.

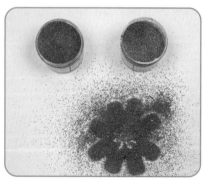

3. Sprinkle the second color onto the glue, then repeat with additional desired colors.

4. Make certain not to "pour" the glitter onto the glue, or the remaining glitter colors will not adhere.

Designer Note: Try not to create definite lines with one color of glitter, as this will cause the second color to meet the line of the first color, not blend with it.

A Card for All Occasions

There are a number of reasons to send someone a card. Holidays, birthdays, or just to let someone know you're thinking of them. Here are a few ideas to get you started:

Special Occasions:
birthdays, engagements, weddings, new babies, anniversaries

Holidays:
Valentine's Day, Saint Patrick's Day, Easter, Mother's Day, Father's Day, Independence Day, Halloween, Thanksgiving, Hanukkah, Christmas, New Year's

Designer Tip:
Not all greeting cards need to have words on the front or inside. If you want to be certain the card recipient knows exactly what message you're trying to convey, then using words are necessary. However, if you want the receiver to create their own meaning, then not using any words may be best.

Miscellaneous:
congratulations (new job, new home, receipt of an award), graduation, moving away, breaking up, meeting someone new, thank you, encouragement, friendship, apology, sickness, a loss

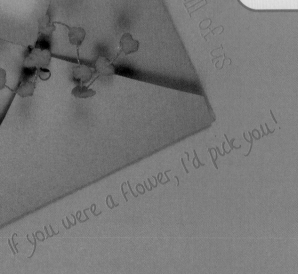

Thanks a Bunch!

Roses are red, violets are blue, these flowers are here because I love you!

From all of us

If you were a flower, I'd pick you!

Designer Tip:
The same card design may be used with different sentiments or for various occasions. For example, everyone loves flowers. Plus they are fun and easy to make from paper, wood, foam shapes, or buttons. They can be plain or patterned; big or small; have centers that are glittered, beaded, buttoned, or shaped with stars, hearts, squares, or triangles.

A Style All Their Own

There are a number of reasons to send the cards you make, and lots of different kinds of people to receive them! All of the people in your life like different things. Here is a list of the types of cards to choose from to make for family and friends that have a style all their own.

Campy: overdone, stylish, mod, hip, clever, perceptive, sophisticated, cosmopolitan, theatrical, exaggerated, extravagant

What to Say:

♥ Passion for Fashion

♥ This is not a dress rehearsal

♥ It's a Jungle out there

Elegant: luxurious, posh, grand, rich, gorgeous, ornamental, excellent, superior, exquisite, tasteful, well-made, sophisticated, stylish, fashionable, cultured, lovely, classical

Funny: amusing, comical, hilarious, entertaining, fun, merry, teasing, joking, playful, laughable, witty, clever, saucy, sassy, curious, peculiar

Cute: delightfully pretty, dainty, created to charm, precious, childlike, delicate, enchanting, darling, joyful, cheerful, enjoyable, pleasing

What to Say:

★ A moment in my arms. Forever in my heart.

★ Sweet Dreams, Sleep Tight, I Love You, Good Night.

★ twinkle twinkle little star, do you know How loved you are?

Inspirational/Motivational: encouragement, spirit, passion, zeal, enthusiasm, excitement, bright, warm, assuring, comforting, spirit, support, strength, insightful, teaching

What to Say:

✿ TAKE FLIGHT!

✿ Go Where you Want To go, Be What you Want To Be.

✿ There is no such thing as an ordinary life

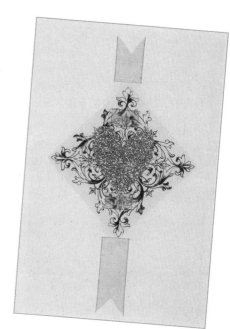

Pretty: pleasing, delightful, lovely, attractive, dainty, delicate, graceful, beautiful

Sentimental: emotional, tender, affectionate, loving, sympathetic, compassionate, romantic, nostalgic

Serious: thoughtful, pensive, reflective, sincere, honest, genuine, real, important, significant, momentous, critical

Basic Materials

Adhesive: A variety of adhesives are used in the projects found in this book. These are: glitter glue; regular white glue that dries clear; glue dots and glue strips (used in scrapbooking); mounting adhesive for projects with large areas of glitter; double-stick tape; transparent tape; specialty glues for foam, metal, or wood; and a small hot-glue gun.

Designer Tips for Adhesives:

★ Use glue that dries clear so that it cannot be seen through glitter.

★ Make sure the tip of your glue bottle is the proper width for the design being drawn. A fine-tip bottle, a small paintbrush or toothpick are best for thin lines and small dots; a medium-tipped bottle is best for thicker lines and medium to large dots; and a flat paintbrush is best for large areas.

★ Practice drawing with the glue bottle before you begin applying glue to artwork.

★ If you make a mistake when applying glue, use a cotton swab to clean glue from surface, or scrape with small piece of cardstock. Allow to dry, then begin again. If glue leaves a visible mark, you will have to extend glittered area, cover with an embellishment, or begin project again.

★ Remember that it is very difficult to draw a perfect line when using glue. If you desire perfection, try using double-stick tape, mounting adhesive, or strips of sticker paper to adhere glitter to paper. Double-stick adhesive strips are available in a variety of widths and sizes, and can be found in the adhesives or scrapbooking section of your local craft store.

Glitter Getter: A Glitter Getter is the perfect tool for catching excess glitter and an easy cleanup! (See page 21)

Miscellaneous: Cotton swabs; mechanical pencil with an eraser; brown kraft paper; paper towels; a hole punch; wire cutters; and ribbons, threads, or strings for tags will also be called for throughout this book.

Mechanical Pencil: Mechanical pencils are best because the lead is very fine and always sharp. The fine lead breaks easily, which will prevent you from applying too much pressure and making the line too dark or causing an indentation on the paper where the pencil mark is.

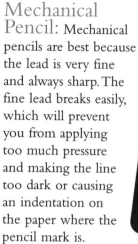

Designer Tip: Always use a pencil to create cutting or placement marks. This way, the lines can be erased so they are not seen on the finished project, and the pencil marks will be much easier to see on darker papers.

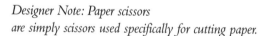

Paintbrushes: A variety of sizes of inexpensive watercolor or art brushes are necessary for applying adhesive and to brush away excess glitter from your card or envelope.

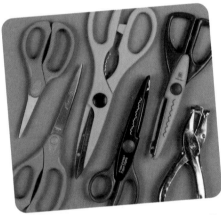

Scissors: Scissors are used for trimming cards to size and for cutting embellishments. You will need very small, pointed scissors; sharp small-sized paper scissors, sharp medium-sized paper scissors; and decorative-edged scissors, such as those used for scrapbooking.

Designer Note: Paper scissors are simply scissors used specifically for cutting paper.

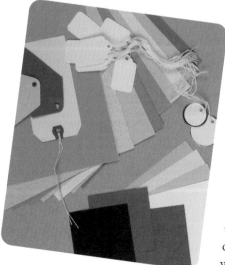

Paper: Regular-weight paper is too flimsy for a card base but it creases easily and makes nice accents for cards. Medium-weight paper is great for making embellishments and envelopes. Miscellaneous patterned, decorative, and handmade paper all make great embellishments for beautiful cards. Heavy-weight or cardstock is used for the greeting card body. It will hold the weight of glued-on objects and will not easily wrinkle when glue is applied.

Ruler: A clear ruler is the easiest ruler to use for making glitter cards but any ruler will work.

Folding Cards

Today cards come in almost every size from tiny gift enclosures to oversized "big" cards. You can choose to make your cards whatever size you want to because it is so easy to make an envelope to match. If you do not wish to make your own envelope then you should choose your envelope first and make your card to fit.

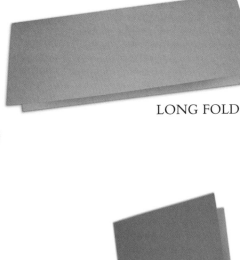

LONG FOLD

GATEFOLD

ACCORDION FOLD

Designer Note: remember if your card is oversized the envelope may take a larger piece of paper than 8½" x 11" so make certain you can find matching paper large enough to create an envelope. In this case you may wish to make a nontraditional envelope without flaps.

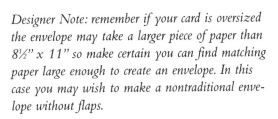

SHORT FOLD

Designer Technique: Folding Your Card

1. Measure card using a ruler and lightly pencil a mark at center.

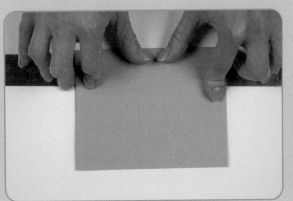

3. Smooth each fold by sliding a pencil or bone folder over crease. If using a pencil, erase any unwanted marks.

2. Place ruler so one long edge is on marked line. Fold one edge of paper over to meet opposite side, matching up corners and holding in place with your middle and index fingers. Place your thumbs in middle of card and crease.

Note: Make certain the fold is tight against ruler. Press down to reinforce the crease working from center of card out to edges.

Designer Technique for Basic Glitter Cards

The basics needed to make even the simplest of cards:

♥ Folded cardstock of choice

♥ Embellishments of choice

♥ Matching envelope

1. Adhere design to card front.
2. Decide areas of design to glitter. *Follow Steps 2–6 for each individual color.*

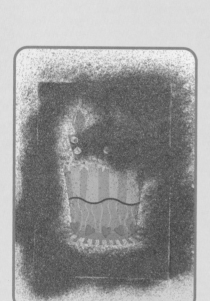

3. Cover larger areas with double-stick tape or mounting adhesive and add glue or adhesive dots in areas where you will be using the same color glitter. Place design on "Glitter Getter" and apply glitter.

Designer Note: Larger, flatter areas should be completed first.

4. Adhere glue dots to smaller areas of design. Do not remove protective backing until ready to glitter. Remove backing and glitter.

IMPORTANT: *Designer Note: If using glue in more than one area, apply different colors of glitter to glued areas one at a time, allowing glue with one color of glitter to dry thoroughly before covering additional areas with glue and adding next color of glitter. For example: apply glue or adhesives to all copper areas, glitter, and let dry. Next apply glue and adhesives to all green areas, glitter, and let dry.*

If you decide not to let the glue dry between the glittering of second, third, or more colors the glitter colors may mix together on the design. If you do not wait for glue to dry between colors be careful not to smear wet glue with your hand while gluing and glittering additional areas and do not shake off excess glitter into "Glitter Getter"* until all colors of glitter have been applied and the glue has dried. This excess glitter in "Glitter Getter" will be mixed and if there are multiple colors combined it may not be able to be used again.

* *Folded sheet of construction paper.*

5. Using a tube or bottle of glue, trace lines or "color in" remaining areas that are to be glittered. (Remember to do this step one color at a time.) Placing your hand against your work surface will help keep it steady. *Note: Begin at the top, left-hand side of page and work your way down and to the right in order to prevent smudging adhesive that has already been applied.*

6. Allow glue to dry. Repeat Steps 2–6 for all remaining colors.

Glitter Idea #1

Glitter Idea #2

Glitter Idea #3

Designer technique for Making a "Glitter Getter"

This is a simple but very important tool when working with glitter. Use a separate Glitter Getter for each color of glitter, and a second sheet of medium weight paper to place under each Glitter Getter.

1. Fold an 8½" x 11", or larger, sheet of paper in half, crease fold. Unfold and lay paper flat on work surface with the crease side down.

2. Apply adhesive to design, place project on Glitter Getter and sprinkle glitter. Leave project on Glitter Getter until adhesive dries.

3. Pick up project and shake off excess glitter.

4. Pick up the sides of Glitter Getter so that glitter falls into the fold.

5. Place edge of crease into glitter container and pour in glitter. Tap the back of Glitter Getter to remove any glitter that may stick to paper. If you miss container and glitter spills, it will fall onto second sheet of medium weight paper. Now pour this spilled glitter back into Glitter Getter.

Embellish!

Scrapbooking supplies: such as rivets; letters and words of all types; charms; stickers; die-cuts; dimensional sticker images; beads; wire, wood, and foam shapes; ribbons; rhinestones; rubber stamps; and almost anything else you find in the scrapbooking aisle can all be used to embellish your cards.

Party supply stores, dollar stores, and super centers all have hundreds of items that can be used in cardmaking. Use your imagination: swizzle sticks can be glittered and glued to a card; confetti can be placed inside the card envelope for added surprise; and small candies can add a sweet treat for the recipient of your card.

Cards can be embellished any way you wish. Use your imagination— the sky is the limit!

Cut-outs

When applying embellishments decide which glue is best for the job. Directions on the adhesive bottle or package will give you the information that you need.

Embellishments

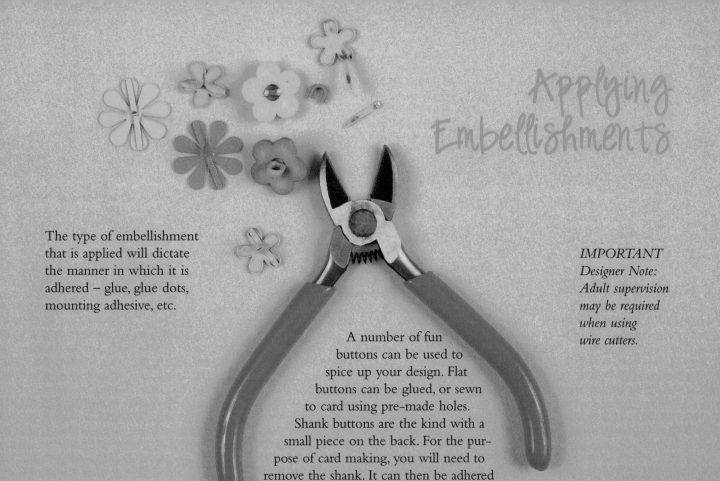

The type of embellishment that is applied will dictate the manner in which it is adhered – glue, glue dots, mounting adhesive, etc.

A number of fun buttons can be used to spice up your design. Flat buttons can be glued, or sewn to card using pre-made holes. Shank buttons are the kind with a small piece on the back. For the purpose of card making, you will need to remove the shank. It can then be adhered with white glue, a glue gun, or glue dots.

IMPORTANT
Designer Note:
Adult supervision may be required when using wire cutters.

Metal, paper, plastic, foam, or wooden numbers, letters, and words are great ways to embellish your cards.

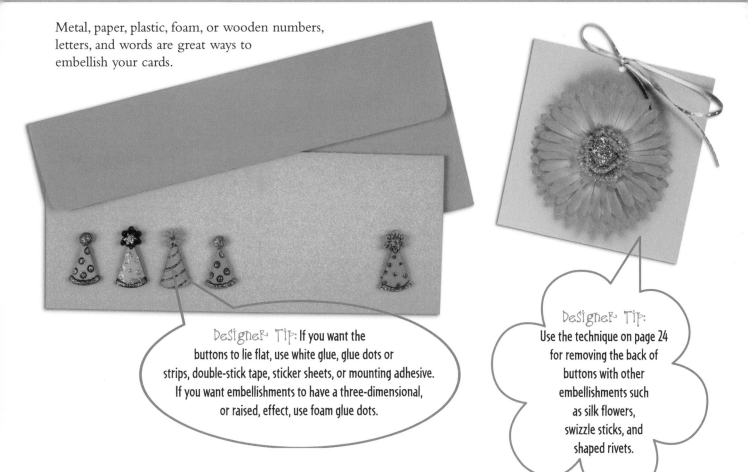

Designer Tip: If you want the buttons to lie flat, use white glue, glue dots or strips, double-stick tape, sticker sheets, or mounting adhesive. If you want embellishments to have a three-dimensional, or raised, effect, use foam glue dots.

Designer Tip: Use the technique on page 24 for removing the back of buttons with other embellishments such as silk flowers, swizzle sticks, and shaped rivets.

Oh So Easy Glitter Cards

Sometimes you just need a fast easy card that is extraordinary. They are fun to think about, to shop for, and oh so simple to make. Buy a non-traditional card embellishment that represents what it is that you want to say, add glitter, glue it to the card front, write a message......or not, and give it away. With a little creativity, your ideas will be endless!

What to say:

 You make everything add up

❋ I Love You X Infinity

❋ You are my #1

What to say:

❋ Congratulations for Crossing the Finish Line!

❋ TRADING PAINT

❋ Start Your Engines

❋ Need for Speed

What to say:

★ Make a Wish

★ Celebrate the Magic

★ A Wishing Wand for You

★ She changes everything she touches

What to say:

♥ What Color is Imagination?

♥ Color me shades of blue . . . without YOU!

♥ for memory has painted this perfect day with colors that never fade (by carrie jacobs bond)

Designer Tip
Use playing cards or pre-school flip cards and pick the numbers that are perfect for the occasion.

What to say:

♥ You're #1

♥ Sweet 16

♥ I Love 50!

♥ It's Crazy to be 8!

♥ Lucky #7

What to say:

❀ If not now when?

❀ Where have you been?

❀ I'm CONFUSED!

❀ Whatever the question is, the answer is no (yes)!

❀ Just because!

❀ Why Not?

❀ Have I ever told you........

What to say:

❀ When will you ever have more time than you do right now?

❀ I HAD THE TIME OF MY LIFE!

❀ There is no time like the present

❀ This day will never come this way again

❀ TIME IS PRECIOUS, SPEND IT WISELY!

❀ Only time will tell

❀ when was the last time you did something for the first time?

What to say:

✱ Celebrate, It's Your Day!

✱ I'm Worth It!

✱ It's Good Being #1

✱ QUEEN FOR A DAY

Designer Tip:
Buy a blue ribbon at a party supply or novelty store, glitter the ribbon tails, then add a pin back. This is a great way to say, "You're number one!"

By the book

What to say:

♥ Your Story Begins Here

♥ Read all about It

What to say:

★ Make a Wish

★ Wish Big

★ It's birthday Time

Close your eyes

so you can see

Celebrate Every Moment

What to say:

✱ Stay Focused

✱ Hey Good Looking!

✱ Looking for Mr. Right....now!

✱ is it true you have to see it to believe it or do you have to believe it before you can see it

The Search for Buried Treasure

A treasure hunt is a fun activity for kids and adults alike—invite your friends to a treasure hunt by creating specially monogrammed cards with their first initial on the front and the party details on the inside.

Create "treasure clues" by glittering the cards that contain the clues and hiding them inside miniature treasure chests. Use white glue to cover desired areas of the treasure chests with glitter.

What to say:

✱ I'm glad I "found" you!

✱ **Ahoy! Keep yer eye on the loot!**

✱ You're a Treasure to Me

Fanfare of Fortune

A sweet gift that anyone can enjoy is a glitzy take-out box of fortune cookies! Simply glitter the designs of your choice, such as hearts and flowers in bright colors, and adhere them to the box. Embellish a card with the same designs, and tuck inside the box before adding the cookies.

If desired, create more glittery shapes and adhere to a brightly colored fan. Crease the shapes so that they bend with the fan folds.

What to say:

★ Great Fortune Will Soon Be Yours...

★ **happy times await you**

★ Good Luck Is On Its Way

★ **You Will Be Famous One Day**

★ from a past misfortune good luck will come to you

> Designer Tip:
> This project also makes a great invitation to a party. Simply tuck an invitation card into the box with the phrase "Accept the Next Proposal You Receive" or "Luck Will Visit You on ......" put the date of the party

Mardi Gras Masquerade

Mardi Gras means fun, celebration, and partying. Simply coat plastic masks in glitter and attach a small tag as a card or party invitation.

Designer Tip:
If you are using regular-sized cards or invitations, try slipping some Mardi Gras beads into the envelope for an added, festive touch.

What to say:

- Celebrate!
- It's Party Time!

Designer Tip:
For picture frames adhere bottom and sides to tag, but leave top open so a photograph can be slipped easily inside.

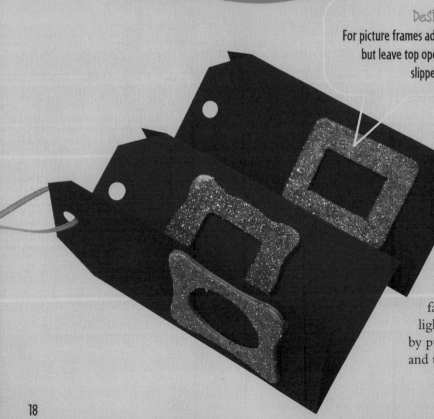

An accordion folded tag with glittered picture frames makes a great party favor. Supply small cameras so that friends can take pictures of each other. On the card glue a frame to first tag then leave every other tag side blank and attach a glittered frame to facing tag.

Guests can add pictures from the party to frames and write in memories of their favorite party moments. Just remember to use light-colored or metallic felt tip pens. Finish off by punching a hole through the top of the tag, and tie with string, ribbon, or Mardi Gras beads.

Caliente Fiesta!

This card is simple to make but so much fun to receive! Cut designs from paper before glittering, or purchase swizzle sticks and cut ends off. Use a paintbrush to apply glue before glittering. Spice up your party decorations with even more glitter, and you're off to a sizzling start.

What to say:

★ you're hot!

★ Party On!

★ VERRRRY HOT!

★ **caliente fiesta!**

★ shake things up!

Designer Tip:
To ensure glitter stays adhered to decorations, try spritzing them with hairspray.

Disco Mania

Whether you're using it as a party invitation or as a card to accompany a gift CD, this design is all-around rockin'!

Cover hearts with mounting adhesive and apply glitter. Include record stickers, shimmery disco balls, or any other desired embellishments!

What to say:

♥ Let's Dance

♥ You Rock!

♥ Do The hustle

♥ And the Beat Goes On...

♥ Another One Bites the Dust

♥ I've Got You Babe

Lucky #7

These fun and fabulous cards are the perfect way to say, "It's your lucky day!" Just glitter the center of three poker chips, or "frame" a playing card with Vegas-worthy glitz.

What to say:

* Lucky You!
* Good Luck!
* It's Your Lucky Day!
* I'm Lucky You Are My Friend

You are #1

Anyone that plays sports will appreciate a good luck card before the big game. Glam up your desired slogan with the same color glitter as the recipient's sports team, and make the inside just as sporty with stickers, ribbons, or any other embellishments.

What to say:

* It ain't over til it's over!
* Take me out to the ballgame
* Practice, Practice, Practice
* Girls Just Want To Win!
* The secret to stardom is the rest of the team (by John Wooden)
* The desire and the will must be stronger than the skill

Hollywood

Want to let someone know they're a star in your life or invite your friends to watch the Oscars? Invite them with an invitation to see the stars! This card says it all.

Designer Note: Stickers, wooden or foam shapes die cuts, or cutout hearts and stars can all be glittered.

What to say:

⭐ **Star Power**

⭐ Star Struck

⭐ YOU ARE A STAR

⭐ "Where Are You Going?" I asked; "To Dance Among the Stars," she said.

⭐ Party With the Stars

⭐ Wish upon a star

What to say:

❤ Queen Me!

❤ Life is Good!

❤ Me, Me, Me!

❤ Princess of quite a lot

❤ Some Days You Just Feel Like a Princess

❤ **It's Good to Be Queen**

❤ It's a Queen Thing

❤ Everyday is a Tiara Day!

Princess

This simple card can be embellished to your royal heart's content! Just adhere glitter to foam, wood, or paper shapes before applying shapes to front of card.

> **Designer Tip:**
> For an extra touch, glue jewels to the points of the crown.

Gifts Galore

Cut a series of squares, making each subsequent square .6 cm smaller than the one preceding it. Glitter each square a different color and adhere to card. Adhere ribbon from top to bottom and from left to right as shown in photograph, finishing with a bow on top.

What to say:

❋ DREAM BIG

❋ You Are a Gift We Celebrate All Year

❋ Good Friends Make Good Gifts

❋ Everyone Has a Gift to Give

❋ Give Me Everything I Want and Nothing I Need

❋ i Want iT all and i Want iT Delivered

❋ Happy Happy Birthday to My Dear Friend

You Light Up My Life

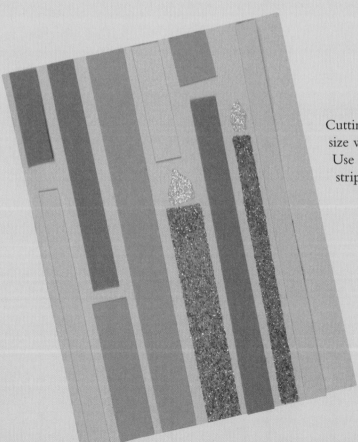

Cutting strips of co-coordinating paper in different size widths and lengths makes this card of candles. Use different sizes of double stick tape to adhere strips, glitter whichever candles and flames you like.

What to say:

❋ Memories are simply moments that refuse to be ordinary

❋ How old would you be if you didn't know how old you were?

Shop 'til you drop!

These tiny shopping bags can be cut from plain or printed papers, adhere a handle made from string or thread, and then add glitter.

What to say:

♥ CaRRied away?!

♥ too much of everything is never enough!

♥ Gotta Have It! Want It! Need It!

♥ Retail Therapy

♥ Let's Shop!

IT'S in The bag!

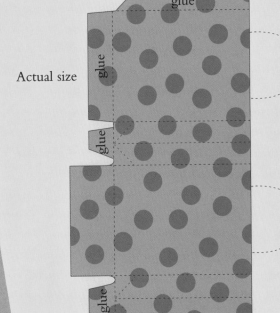

Actual size

glue · glue · glue · glue · glue

A Gift for You

23

Be Everyone You Are!

The clothing patterns used in this design can be funky, fun, or fancy; kitschy or traditional; for adults, teens, or babies… Just use your imagination!

What to say:

❋ Trust Yourself

❋ The Life You Lead Should Be the Life You Love

❋ Live Like You Mean It!

❋ Elegance Is an Attitude!

❋ When Was the Last Time You Did Something for the First Time?

• What do you pack to pursue your dreams
❋ and what do you leave behind?

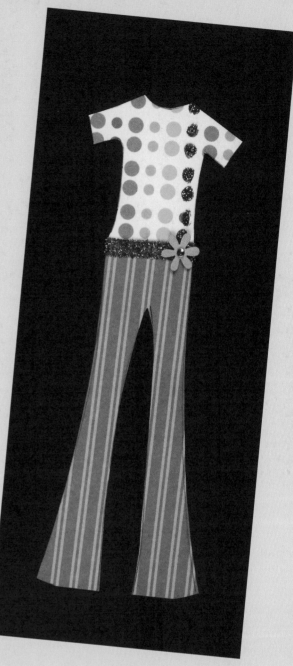

Designer Tip:
A fun touch for this card is to extend the skirt or the pant legs down past the bottom edge of card. Make certain your envelope is large enough to accommodate design without bending it.

24

Call of the wild!

Some say, "You are what you wear!" and even though that may not always be true, your clothes can definitely speak a thousand words about what you like and who you are. So if you want to change your life for a day, change your clothes….especially your shoes! Now, you can be anyone you want to be.

Card Phrases:

★ Everything is Sweetened by Risk (by Alexander Smith)

★ The world of reality has its limits, the world of imagination is boundless. (by Rousseau)

★ "Goodbye", she said, "I'm off to join the CIRCUS! (by Leigh Standley)

Party Hats

These party hats make a great invitation or thank you card for a party recently attended. Just draw hat pattern to the desired size, cut and fold pattern on dotted line, then glitter!

Designer Tip:
Top the hats with a pom-pom, rhinestone, or button.

Attach pom-pom

Hat pattern

Rim pattern

Card Phrases:

★ It's Party Time!

★ Celebrate! It's Your Day

25

Purseonality!

What is a girl without her purse?! We all want more than one, we all need more than one, we all have to have more than one!

Card Phrases:

✿ You're Worth It!

✿ the day you were born the world had to make room for a little more fancy (by Leigh Standley)

✿ YOU GO GIRL!

✿ sHOPPORTUnist!

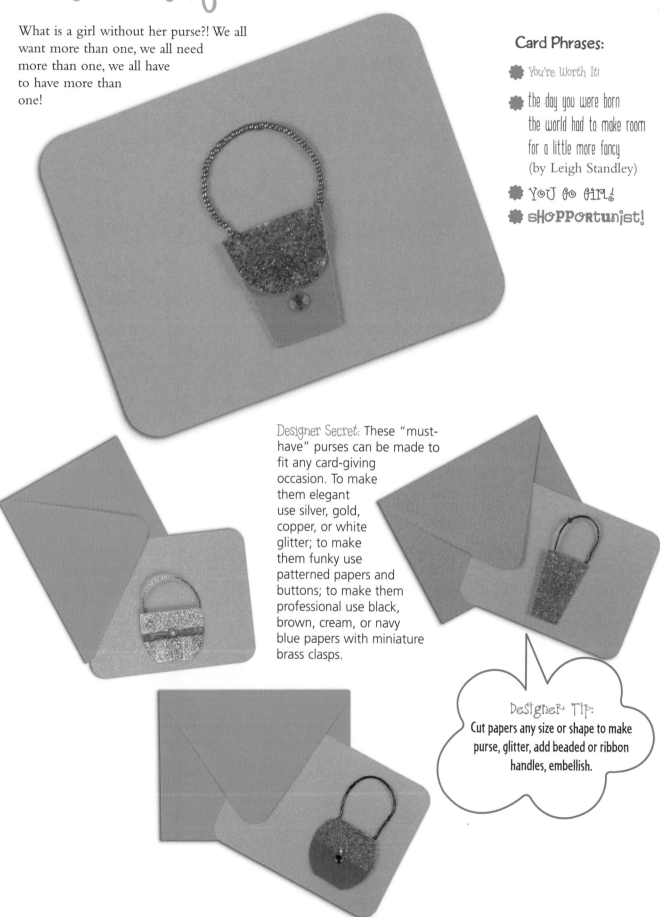

Designer Secret: These "must-have" purses can be made to fit any card-giving occasion. To make them elegant use silver, gold, copper, or white glitter; to make them funky use patterned papers and buttons; to make them professional use black, brown, cream, or navy blue papers with miniature brass clasps.

Designer Tip:
Cut papers any size or shape to make purse, glitter, add beaded or ribbon handles, embellish.

Bee Yourself!

Card Phrases:

✿ Beelieve

✿ Bee Everything You Are

✿ Bee Happy!

✿ Thank you for beeing my friend

✿ Beelieve in Yourself

✿ Bee a Dreamer

✿ JUST BEELIEVE

Did you know that according to the principles of aerodynamics bees shouldn't be able to fly? No one ever told them they couldn't do it, so they just do!

English Cracker Cards

These "crackers" are tubes that can hold a scroll card as well as a tiny treasure. In Victorian times, crackers were given at Christmas parties and contained a charm, a joke, and a tissue paper crown. When the ends were pulled, a friction spot on the inside would snap, creating the cracking noise. While our crackers will not make a noise, as the snaps are difficult to find, they are still fun to make, fun to give, and fun to receive!

Designer Technique:

1. Measure the length of a toilet paper tube, adding 2" (5cm) to each end.

2. Measure the circumference of the tube, add 2" (5cm).

3. Using dimensions, cut two layers of brightly colored plain paper.

4. Cover tissue paper tube with strips of double-stick tape.

5. Place a line of double-stick tape down long edge of cut paper.

6. Place paper tube onto paper opposite line of double-stick tape. Roll paper onto tube, smoothing as you go.

7. Tie one end with string or ribbon. Fill cracker with desired objects, then tie the other end.

8. Glitter crackers.

Stepping Out

The mood of this fashion-forward card will be changed depending on the paper you choose to use. Glitter against black paper will make this look like a party shoe, while brown paper creates more of a business shoe. Yellow paper with pink flowers will create a summer shoe perfect for a luncheon invitation. The shoe on this card can be made to match just about any occasion you can think of!

Something Old
Something New,
Something Borrowed...
and Great Shoes!

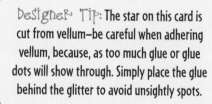

Designer Tip: The star on this card is cut from vellum—be careful when adhering vellum, because, as too much glue or glue dots will show through. Simply place the glue behind the glitter to avoid unsightly spots.

Card Phrases:

★ One Shoe Can Change Your Life...by Cinderella

★ I'm late, I'm late for a very important date!

★ Lost: one glass slipper by Cinderella

★ SOME DAYS YOU JUST HAVE TO DANCE

★ Put on your dancing shoes

★ Here is to world peace and cute shoes

It's Your Lucky Day!

Card Phrases:

❋ Find Your Own Luck

❋ Best of Luck!

❋ The harder you work the luckier you get

Two Hearts, One Love

Card Phrases:

♥ 1 + 1 = US

♥ I will love you forever, for always

♥ **Forever Us**

♥ My heart reminds me

♥ Love is in the air

♥ This is where I belong

♥ Love you, Sooo much

♥ Friend to Friend, Heart to Heart

Hearts, every time you see one it is like seeing it for the first time!

Ready-Made Tags

These tags are so simple; you can make them in minutes. Purchase a tag or card from your favorite store, spice it up with glitter and embellishments!

Designer Tip:
Make a cute beaded ring for the envelope by taking a thin piece of wire, string plastic beads, and twist the ends of wire together.

Mirror, Mirror On The Wall

In Victorian times men put tiny mirrors in the cards that they gave to their lady friends so that she could "see" who he loved. Today, cute cards with mirrors can be given by anyone, to anyone, for any reason.

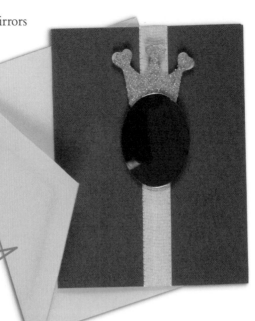

Designer Tip:
Small round, square, or oval mirrors can be found in craft and hobby stores. To make this card put a ribbon down the middle of the page using double stick tape, cut out a crown, glitter, adhere with dimensional glue dot, add a mirror, and write your message.

Card Phrases:

❀ You Go Girl!

❀ It's all about me!

❀ More than a pretty face

❀ Mirror, mirror on the wall. I am my mother after all!

❀ **Smile, it confuses people.**

❀ Let me be the princess!

❀ When you believe in yourself, everything is possible.

❀ Be yourself, everyone else is taken

Imagine

Not all cards have to be traditional. This one is a small book that can be used as a sketchbook, scrapbook, or a storybook.

Designer Tip:
Make the inside of your card as "pretty" as the outside. When you tape a picture on the inside, frame it with paper, ribbon, or glitter so there are no raw edges showing.

Designer Technique:

1. To make a 4"-square book, cut pages 4" x 8". Stack pages together, fold and crease in half. Make the cover by cutting cardstock to ½" larger than the book pages on all sides. Cut square, or other desired shape, in center of cover. Staple cover and pages together along crease line. Glitter border on cut window of card front by using strips of double-stick tape.

2. Fit desired photograph behind opening, adhere using tape, finish edges. Write desired message on first page, and fit into matching envelope.

Chapter 3... Don't Forget the Envelope!

Envelopes are the frosting on the cake, the finishing touch, the *piece de resistance*! Sometimes, the envelope can be as important as the card. It is the first "word" of your message, which renders a plain, white envelope beneath you!

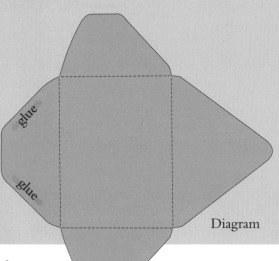

glue

glue

Diagram

Designer Technique:

Here are a few basics for creating envelopes as fabulous as your cards:

1. Measure card and add ¼" to 1" on all sides. If there are embellishments that will push the envelope outward, make certain to accommodate for this with a larger envelope.

2. Lightly sketch outline for envelope onto the center of a sheet of medium-weight paper. Add one flap for each side, as well as top and bottom flaps. See diagram for inspiration!

3. Cut out shape.

4. Fold and crease flaps, using ruler as a guide.

5. Apply glue strips, double-stick tape, or adhesive to small side flaps. Fold and smooth. Repeat with bottom flap.

6. Decorate envelope as desired.

XOXO

Designer Technique:

1. Cut and fold cardstock.

2. Trim edge with decorative-edged scissors, then fold and adhere flaps.

3. Punch hole and thread ribbon through as shown in photograph. Add button or bead, if desired, and tie a bow.

4. Glitter message, insert card, and voila! Your card is complete!

Designer Tip: If this envelope is going to be mailed it must be placed into a traditional mailing envelope.

Party Glam tubes

Designer Secret: Fill tubes with the recipient's favorite candy as well as a note.

Designer Tip: If these are to be mailed they will have to be placed in a mailing tube or box.

These party tubes can be purchased at party supply, craft, and novelty stores. Wrap double stick tape around tubes, glitter, embellish, fill with letter rolled into a scroll, replace end cap, and give.

Let's Do Lunch!

These cute little lunch boxes can be found in party supply and novelty stores.

Glitter a large flower shape of choice. String alphabet beads to read: Let's Do Lunch on a thin wire. Make the wire long enough to thread into the back hinge and into the inside of the lunch box. Place small glue dots on the back of every other bead to hold them in place. Place invitation in lunchbox with treats, and you have an offer that nobody can refuse!

Party Bags Designer Technique:

1. Use die-cut butterfly, fold on dotted lines, glitter butterfly body.

2. Take a purchased pinwheel, cut stick length of bag, paint stick with glue and glitter, attach to bag with glue gun.

3. Make a small tag and envelope, punch a hole, tie with colored threads, and attach to bag. Use candle button as a closure.

IMPORTANT
Designer Note: Adult supervision may be required when using glue gun.

Paper Party Bags

These colorful bags can be purchased in several sizes and colors at craft, paper, or party supply stores.

EASY FUN PROJECTS WITH

Newspapers, Magazines, & Catalogs

Jo Packham

**Easy Fun Projects with
Newspapers, Magazines & Catalogs**
by Jo Packham

© 2007 by
Mud Puddle Books, Inc.
54 W. 21st Street
Suite 601
New York, NY 10010
info@mudpuddlebooks.com

ISBN: 978-1-60311-122-5

Printed in China

Table of Contents

Working with the pages of old newspapers, magazines, books, and catalogs can be more fun than buying scrapbook paper any day. Begin saving a select few newspapers—those with great pictures, stories that interest you, the funny papers, etc; and do the same with books, catalogs, and magazines. Tear out the pages that you think you will use someday, store them in a box, and throw the rest away. On days when you can't find anything to do, cut special words and pictures from the pages that you have saved and put them in envelopes so that you will be ready when you start your projects.

Remember when you work with newspaper that the ink will rub off, so you should not wear white or light-colored clothing and you should work on a plastic surface. This is especially true when using découpage glue.

There are a few techniques you need to know before starting some of the projects in this book. Découpage, for example, means to decorate something with paper cutouts. Simply glue the paper cutouts you wish to use onto your art project. It's as simple as that!

Another technique you might be not be familiar with is how to use a cool-temperature glue gun to adhere parts of your project together. Always remember to ask a grown-up to help you, because even cool-temperature glue can be dangerous if used without proper adult supervision.

Important: All papers used in this book, unless otherwise stated, were pages taken from old newspapers, magazines, and catalogs.

Newspaper projects can be large or small, silly or serious, but always fun and easy. One very fun project for using small pieces of paper and storing the little stuff you love are Matchbox Treasure Boxes. Using double-stick tape, simply cover small or large empty matchboxes with paper and embellishments. Fill the insides with folded paper books, pieces of paper, miniature tags, envelopes, or recipe cards. Add a miniature toy, treat, or message. Keep some, give some to family and friends, but have fun making hundreds!

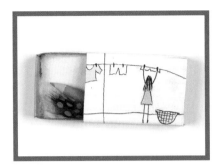

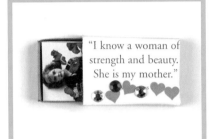

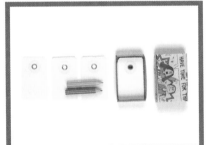

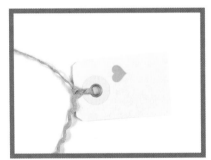

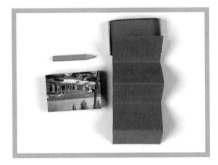

Picture Perfect

What you need:

- Paper
- Decorative-edged scissors
- Découpage or white glue
- Double-stick tape
- Letters that spell MOM
- Mom's favorite photo of you
- Paintbrush
- Photo holder (you can bend one out of wire or buy one at your local craft store)
- Piece of cardstock
- Screw or drill
- Square block of wood
- Wood glue or epoxy

Instructions

1. Using double-stick tape, mount photograph onto cardstock. Trim edges with decorative-edged scissors.

2. Découpage paper pieces onto 5 sides of wooden block.

3. With screw or drill and a grown-up's help, drill a small hole into the center of one side of the block of wood.

4. Bend photo holder, dip in wood glue, and screw into hole.

Mom's Wish Jar

What you need:

- Letters that spell "I love you, Mom"
- Paper strip
- Double-stick tape
- Jar or bottle with lid
- Pencil
- Red paper
- Scissors
- Ultra-fine permanent black marker

Instructions

1. Cut strips of red paper, write wishes to your mom with black marker, then roll paper around pencil.

2. Cut letters that spell "I love you, Mom" and adhere to jar.

3. Fill jar with wishes and adhere long paper strip over lid to act as a seal.

Mom's Banner

What you need:

- Paper
- Decorative-edged scissors
- Double-stick tape
- Letter stickers
- Long, thin ribbon

Instructions

1. Using decorative-edged scissors, cut circles of desired size from paper.

2. Fold circles in half, crease, and lay open on tabletop.

3. Put a piece of double-stick tape on each circle at crease.

4. Lay ribbon over tape. Fold circles over and crease.

5. Put letter stickers on half circles to spell a message to Mom.

6. Hang where Mom will see it.

Purses and Pictures for Mom

Instructions

1. Cut 2 identical purse shapes from cardstock. Set one aside and cut a viewing window through which photograph will be seen in the second.

2. Découpage paper pieces onto purse shape. Embellish as desired.

3. Use a length of ribbon or a beaded wire to serve as purse handle and glue to the back of the purse frame. Trim photo 1" (2.5 cm) larger than window. Tape photo edges to back of frame.

4. Cover back of frame with double-stick tape. Adhere second piece of cardstock to finish frame back.

5. On back of frame, write who, what, when, and where about the picture, as well as when and why you gave it to your Mom.

What you need:

- Paper
- Cardstock
- Découpage or white glue
- Double-stick tape
- Embellishments
- Cool-temperature glue gun/ glue sticks
- Paintbrush
- Photograph
- Ribbon or beaded wire
- Scissors
- Ultra-fine permanent black marker

"What Will I Do for You Today?" Box

What you need:

- Paper
- Cool-temperature glue gun/glue sticks
- Decorative-edged scissors
- Découpage or white glue
- Large bead or knob
- Paintbrush
- Papier mâché box
- Pencil
- Strips of plain paper
- Ultra-fine marker

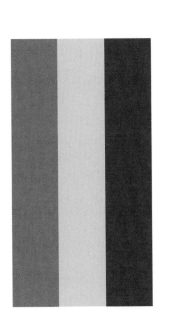

Instructions

1. Découpage paper pieces to box and lid. *Note: If you cannot find a phrase on a page that you like, write one with stickers or a pen.*

2. Glue bead to lid to act as a handle.

3. Trim edges of plain paper with decorative-edged scissors

4. On each plain paper strip, write one job that you will do for your mom on a daily basis. Curl strip around a pencil, then put strips in box. Close lid and give to Mom just to say thank you.

Roses For You

What you need:

- Paper
- Cool-temperature glue gun/ glue sticks
- Craft paint: black and red
- Decorative-edged scissors
- Paintbrushes
- Pencil
- Scissors
- Small binder clip
- Stapler
- Unglazed terra cotta flowerpot and saucer
- Wooden knob

Note: You can use craft paint or paints specially manufactured for use on terra cotta.

Instructions

1. Paint knob black. Paint pot and saucer red. Let dry thoroughly. *Note: You may need several coats of paint.*

2. Cut several 4" (10.2 cm) squares from paper, making sure some have red ink on them.

3. Fold squares into fourths. Going from corner to corner of each square, draw a quarter-circle and cut out with decorative-edged scissors.

10

4 Clamp small binder clip onto folded "rose petal."

5 Staple corner of petal.

6 Remove clip and "open" petals.

7 Glue roses around pot, just under the rim.

8 Glue large knob to bottom of saucer. Now it's a lid with a handle!

Welcome Sign

What you need:

- Paper
- Découpage or white glue
- Paintbrush
- Wooden door hanger (can be purchased at your local craft or hobby store)

Instructions

1. Select pictures and phrases from the paper that have something to do with your pet.

2. Découpage a collage of these images onto the door hanger.

3. Hang on the outside of your door!

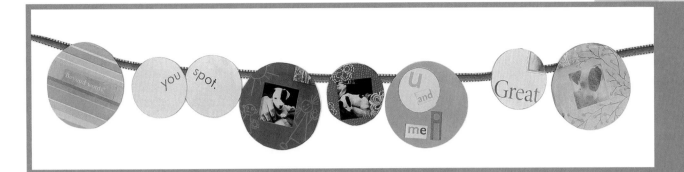

It's a Banner Day!

Instructions

1. Cut several circles of desired sizes from cardstock or file folders. Make sure to cut 2 circles of each size. Using decorative-edged scissors, cut circles of the same sizes from paper.

2. Using double-stick tape, cover one side of each cardstock circle with a paper image.

3. Lay half the circles down on the tabletop at desired intervals, and cover the plain sides with double-stick tape.

4. Lay ribbon over the circles.

What you need:

- Paper
- Cardstock or file folders
- Decorative-edged scissors
- Double-stick tape or scrapbooking adhesives
- Ribbon
- Scissors

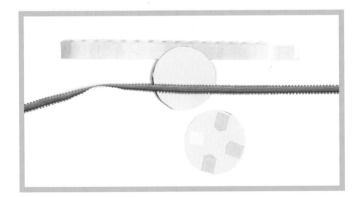

5. Adhere two circles together with ribbon in-between.

6. Hang banner where your pet will know that it's for him!

"Good Boy!"

What you need:

- Paper
- Decorative-edged scissors
- Double-stick tape
- Favorite pet pictures
- Small lunch sacks

Instructions

1. Using decorative-edged scissors, cut around your pet's picture. Cut a handle for the sack from printed paper.

2. Using double-stick tape, tape handle into place on lunch sack, then tape photo under handle.

3. Fill with goodies for you or your pet!

Doggie Treats

What you need:

- Paper
- Decorative-edged scissors
- Double-stick tape
- Favorite pet pictures
- Small cans
- Treats

Instructions

1. Using decorative-edged scissors, cut around your pet's picture and cut a strip from printed paper.

2. Fill can with treats.

3. Using double-stick tape, tape paper strip over top of can, then tape photo over strip. Whether the treats inside the can are for you or man's best friend, it will make the gift much more special.

Message Board

Make special thumbtacks for everyone you know!

What you need:

- Paper
- Corkboard memo boards
- Découpage or white glue
- Large specialty thumbtacks (Found in office supply stores)
- Paintbrush
- Scissors

Instructions

1. Cut paper circles to approximately twice the size of the thumbtack surface.

2. Découpage paper circles onto surface.

3. Use your personalized thumbtacks on your corkboard to display messages, hang pictures, or tack up anything you like!

Dinner At 8!

What you need:

- Paper
- Découpage or white glue
- Drinking straws
- Paintbrush
- Pen, pencil, or skewer
- Scissors

Instructions

1. Cut paper into triangular shape. The base of the triangle should measure the length you want the placemat to be.

2. Place drinking straw at the tip of the paper triangle, and roll paper around straw.

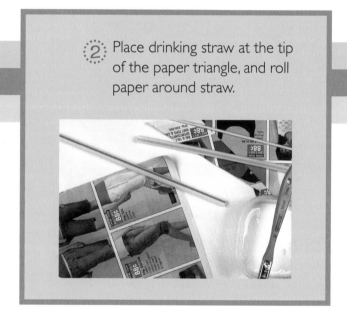

3. When straw is partially covered with paper, spread some glue onto the paper as you roll to secure. Do not get any glue on the straw.

4. When you are finished rolling the paper around the straw, spread glue along the edge and securely wrap paper.

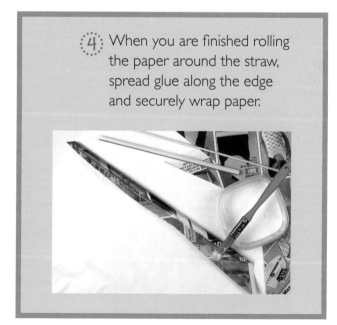

5. Pull the straw through the tube and remove. *Note: You may have to push straw through paper with a pencil or skewer.*

6. Use the pen to press each tube flat, working from the center to each end.

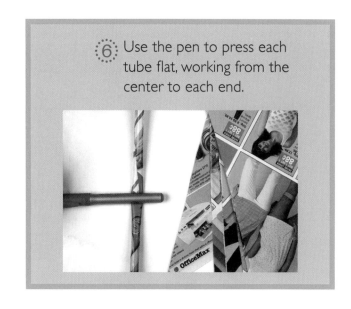

7. Once you have several tubes rolled and flattened, you will weave the tubes together. Lay 3 flattened tubes side-by-side on tabletop, and weave 3 more tubes through them as shown.

8. Continue weaving until the placemat is the size you want it to be. *Note: You can découpage woven placemat so that it will be easier to clean.*

Light Covers

What you need:

- Paper
- Craft knife
- Découpage or white glue
- Embellishments
- Light switch cover
- Paintbrush
- Scissors

Instructions

1. Cut paper rectangle approximately 2" (5.1 cm) larger than light switch cover.

2. Coat front of light switch cover with découpage glue. Place paper face down on tabletop, and set cover in the center of rectangle. Smooth paper over light switch cover from center to edges.

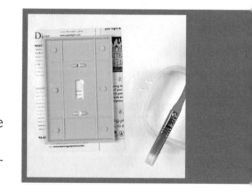

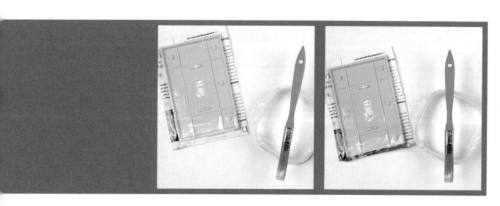

3. Cover one back-side edge of cover with glue and fold paper over.

4 Continue around all 4 sides.

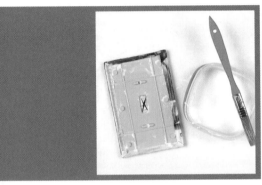

5 With the craft knife, cut an X from corner to corner in space where switch will go. Ask a grown-up for help using the craft knife.

6 Spread glue around hole, fold back corners, and smooth.

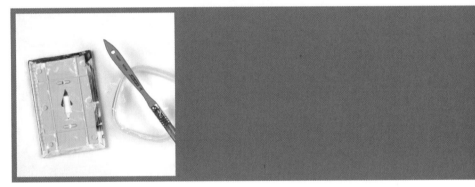

7 Coat the front of the light switch cover with découpage glue and let dry. Repeat several times. This will keep the light switch cover from becoming worn with use.

8 Embellish cover as desired.

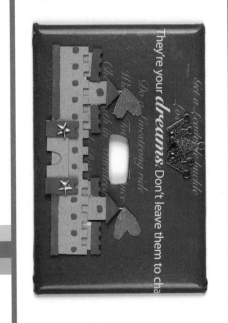

Pencil Holder

What you need:

- Paper
- Découpage or white glue
- Drinking straws
- Masking tape
- Paintbrush
- Pencil or skewer
- Ribbons
- Scissors
- Tall glass jar

Instructions

1. Cut paper into triangular shape. Long edge of triangle should measure 4'' (10.2 cm) longer than the height of the jar.

2. Place straw on tip of triangle and begin to roll.

3. Continue to roll.

4. When you reach the end of the paper, spread glue, roll straw, and press paper edges with your fingers.

5. Remove straw. You may have to push it through with a pencil or a skewer.

6. Make enough tubes to go around jar. Cut ends from tubes.

7. Lay a long strip of masking tape on the table, sticky side up, and place end of tubes along tape. *Note: You may have to tape ends onto table to secure strip.*

8. Continue until you have laid down enough tubes to go around jar.

9. Cover outside of jar with découpage glue, place tube "sheet" onto jar, and wrap ribbon around to hold in place.

10. Cut ends of tubes to be even with top and bottom of jar.

11. Let découpage glue dry thoroughly.

12. Remove holding ribbon and add decorative ribbon on top and bottom of holder. *Note: In place of decorative ribbon, decorative tapes could be used.*

Paperweight

What you need:

- Paper
- Decorative-edged scissors
- Découpage or white glue
- Paintbrush
- Rock
- Scissors
- Ric Rac* (optional)
- Stickers (optional)

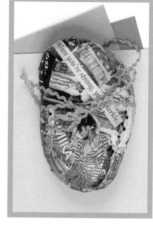

*A narrow zigzag ribbon used as trimming.

Instructions

1. Cut pictures from paper. *Note: You can cut small pieces with decorative-edged scissors so they look like stamps.*

2. Découpage pictures onto rock.

Optional: For a designer touch, you can tie Ric Rac around your rock or embellish with stickers.

Bookmarks

What you need:

- Paper
- Cardstock
- Double-stick tape
- Personal picture
- Scissors

Instructions

1. Cut 2 sheets of cardstock in shape of bookmark with a window for a picture in one bookmark shape only.

2. Cover one side of both pieces of cardstock with double-stick tape. Add images and words cut from paper.

3. Place picture behind window, then stick in place with tape.

4. Using double-stick tape, press blank sides of cardstock together to create bookmark.

Decorative Mats

Instructions

1. Follow Steps 1 through 6 under Dinner at 8! on page 16.

2. Begin to roll first flattened tube into a circle.

3. After you have the center started, pinch the circle into a square.

4. Spread glue one small section at a time as you go.

5. Continue rolling until desired size is reached. *Note: When one tube ends and you need to add another, simply apply extra glue, and butt the new tube against the end of the last tube.*

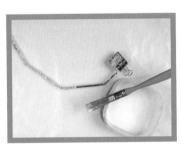

What you need:

- Paper
- Découpage or white glue
- Drinking straws
- Paintbrush
- Pen, pencil, or skewer
- Scissors

Key Chain

What you need:

- Paper
- Double-stick tape
- Hole punch
- Key ring
- Manila tags (from office supply store)
- Markers
- Scissors

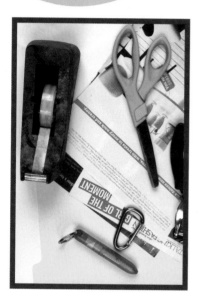

Instructions

1. Cut images from paper to cover tags.

2. Cover one side of tags with double-stick tape and press images in place. Punch hole in each tag.

3. On backside of tag write personal information: name, address, phone number, contact person, etc.

4. Add tags to key ring.

Notebook

What you need:

- Paper
- Composition notebook
- Double-stick tape
- Embellishments
- Scissors

Instructions

1. Cover the composition notebook cover with double-stick tape.
2. Collage favorite images from paper onto cover.
3. Add embellishments.
4. Put words, phrases, images, etc. on inside pages.

Clipboard

Your clipboard can be functional or decorative—use it to write important memos or just keep in your room for show!

What you need:

- Paper
- Clipboard
- Double-stick tape
- Embellishments
- Scissors

Instructions

1. Cut images from paper. Put double-stick tape on the back of the images and collage onto clipboard.
2. Add embellishments as desired.

Journal

Keeping a small journal for every year that you go to school is a fun way to remember what you did and who your friends were. Don't forget to date the pictures and write down your stories—it seems like you will always remember… but you won't!

What you need:

- Paper
- Colored cardstock
- Double-stick tape
- Hole punch
- Ribbon
- Scissors

Instructions

1. Cut colored cardstock to the size you want your journal pages to be.

2. Punch holes in the left side of each page.

3. Tie ribbon through holes.

4. Collage cover with images that are indicative of what the journal is about.

5. Add images and stories to each page.

Envelope Scrapbooks

What you need:

- Paper
- Double-stick tape
- Hole punch
- Large envelopes
- Markers
- Ribbon
- Scissors

Make as many of these fun envelopes as you wish, filling with memorabilia from vacations, birthday parties, the last day of school, or any other event you can think of!

Instructions

1. Cut images from paper that remind you of what you want to record and remember, then adhere to envelope front.

2. Punch hole in envelope below flap. *Note: Hole should be punched here so that envelope can be opened easily.*

3. Put double-stick tape on back of images. Collage images onto envelope front.

4. Write on back what, when, where, and who.

5. Fill envelope with memorabilia.

6. Tie envelopes together with ribbon.

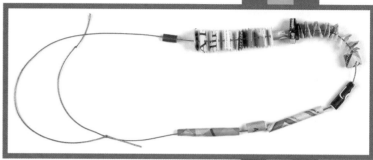

Rolled Beads

What you need:

- Paper
- Découpage or white glue
- Drinking straws
- Paintbrush
- Scissors

Instructions

1. Cut strips of paper to the length of a magazine or newspaper page and the width that you want your beads to be.

2. Cut triangular shapes so the longest side is the length you want the bead to be.

3. Cover the paper strips and triangles with glue.

4. Place the straw at the end of a paper strip or the tip of a triangle, and begin rolling.

5. When you reach the end, apply a little more glue to secure. Let dry completely.

6. Cut straw at bead ends.

7. For additional beads, cut strips of paper, fold accordion-style, punch hole in center of folded strip, string onto necklace with rolled beads.

Tube Bracelets

What you need:

- Paper
- Cool-temperature glue gun/ glue sticks
- Double-stick tape
- Embellishments such as ribbons, buttons, stickers, etc.
- Paper towel tube
- Scissors

Instructions

1. Cut a slit from one end of the paper towel tube to the other.

2. Cut tube into pieces that are the desired width of bracelet. *Note: 2"–2½"(5.1 cm – 6.4 cm) works well.*

3. Cut paper into pieces that you want to collage onto your bracelets.

4. Cover bracelets with double-stick tape and collage with paper pieces.

5. Adhere desired embellishments with glue.

Rolled Paper Necklace

What you need:

- Paper
- Embroidery floss or thread
- Scissors
- Thin ribbon
- Wooden beads

1. Cut paper to the full length you want your beads to be by about 11" (27.9 cm) wide.

2. Place wooden beads in a line, about 2" (5.1 cm) from one edge of paper strip.

3. Begin rolling beads inside paper, tying floss between each bead. *Note: Be careful when rolling the first few beads, as the beads might roll off the paper.*

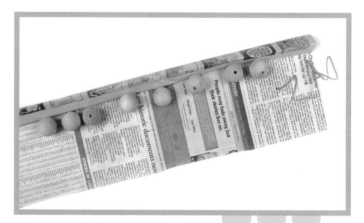

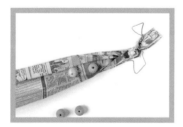

4. Continue rolling and tying as shown.

5. Tie ribbon onto ends of necklace.

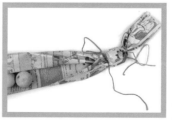

Ring

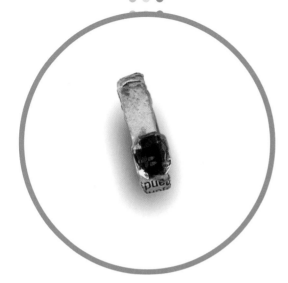

What you need:

- Paper
- Cool-temperature glue gun/glue sticks
- Découpage or white glue
- Drinking straw
- Paintbrush
- Rhinestone with flat side
- Round pen
- Scissors

Instructions

1. Cut paper into triangular shape. The base of the triangle should measure the width you want your ring to be.
2. Place drinking straw at the tip of the paper triangle, and roll paper around straw.
3. Adhere paper as you roll, making sure not to get any glue on the straw.
4. Let dry. Pull straw out of paper tube.
5. Use the pen to press the tube flat, working from center to end.
6. Roll flattened tube into a circle to fit your finger.
7. Glue rhinestone to ring and enjoy!

Wrapped Package

Jewelry must be given in style! Wrap packages with papers the recipient would love. You can also add a little something on top that you love!

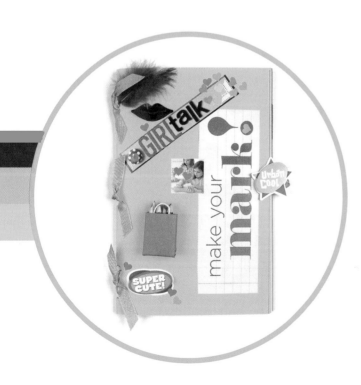

EASY FUN PROJECTS WITH

Cardboard & Tubes

Stephanie, Parker, and Regan Christiansen

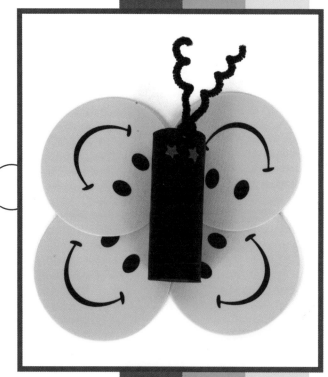

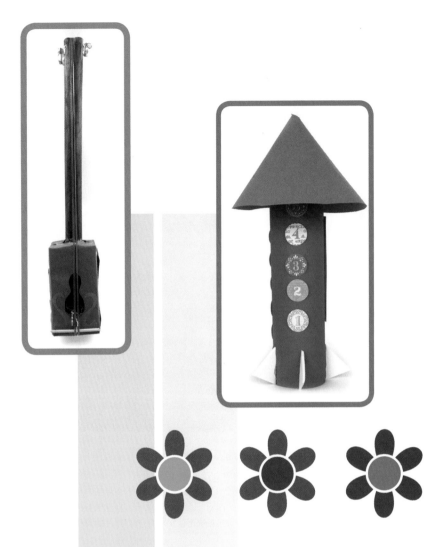

**Easy Fun Projects with
Cardboard & Tubes**

by Stephanie, Parker and Regan Christiansen

© 2007 by
Mud Puddle Books, Inc.
54 W. 21st Street
Suite 601
New York, NY 10010
info@mudpuddlebooks.com

ISBN: 978-1-60311-120-1

Printed in China

Table of Contents

INTRODUCTION

Everyone knows that having paper towels and toilet tissue around the house is a necessity. But who knew making projects from the cardboard tubes that are left over could be so much fun?

By following the easy instructions in this chapter, you can make a number of fun projects to supplement all of your imaginative adventures! From a pretend camera for snapping photographs in the jungle to maracas for heading up your own Mariachi band, you can create just about anything you want.

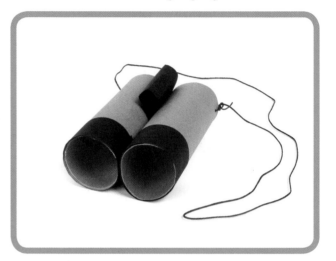

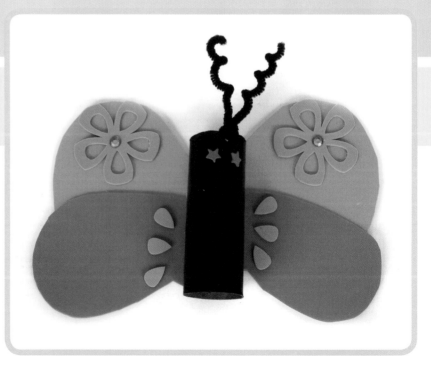

Because cardboard is somewhat thick, it can be difficult to cut through. The projects might call for scissors or a craft knife in order to get the cuts just right. Whenever you need help cutting, especially with sharp, pointy scissors or a craft knife, ask a grown-up to help you.

You might also be required to use a cool-temperature glue gun. A cool-temperature glue gun is just as effective as a hot glue gun, even though it does not warm up quite as much. However, it is still very important that you ask a grown-up to help you when you are using a glue gun of any sort—you don't want to burn your fingers!

As with all craft projects, the most important thing to remember is to have fun! Be as creative as you like and use your imagination. The projects listed here are fun, easy, and great for getting you started, but your imagination is the limit!

Bracelets

Instructions

1. Slit toilet paper tube lengthwise from end to end.

2. Cut toilet paper tube to desired width of bracelet, usually 2–3" (5.1–7.6 cm).

3. Cover bracelet with acrylic paint or aluminum foil, depending on desired look for bracelet.

4. Glue embellishments or sequins onto bracelet and allow to dry.

What you need:

- Cardboard toilet paper tube
- Acrylic paint or aluminum foil
- Craft glue
- Scissors
- Sequins or other desired embellishments
- Sponge (optional, for painting)

Party Poppers

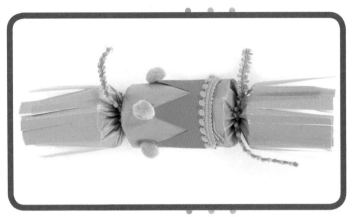

What you need:

- Cardboard toilet paper tube
- Candy or small party favors
- Curling ribbon
- Markers or stickers
- Scissors
- Tissue paper
- Transparent tape

Instructions

1. Cut a piece of tissue paper to 12" (30.5 cm) square.

2. Center the toilet paper tube on the tissue paper. Tape one edge of the tissue paper onto the cylindrical portion of the tube.

3. Roll the toilet paper tube tightly into the tissue paper.

4. Twist one end and secure with tape.

5. Fill the other end of the popper with candy or small party favors.

6. Twist open end and secure with tape.

7. Tie ends with curling ribbon.

8. Decorate popper with marker and/or stickers, as desired.

Kaleidoscope

What you need:

- 2 cardboard paper towel tubes
- Aluminum foil
- Craft glue
- Craft jewels or beads
- Flat cardboard
- Heavy construction paper
- Pencil
- Plastic wrap
- Ruler
- Scissors
- Transparent tape

Instructions

1. Measure and cut construction paper to 4½" (11.4 cm) wide by the original length of the paper.

2. Measure and fold the strip of paper lengthwise into three equal parts, so that each portion is 1½" (3.8 cm).

3. Glue aluminum foil to the construction paper, and reinforce the folds. This should create an equilateral (meaning all sides are the same length) triangle. Make sure the aluminum foil is facing inside the triangular tunnel.

4. Slip the triangular tunnel inside the cardboard tube.

5. Trace the cardboard tube on the piece of flat cardboard and cut out.

6. Cut a small hole in the cardboard circle to create the viewfinder. You might be more comfortable asking a grown-up to help you.

7. Glue or tape the circle to one end of your cardboard tube.

8. Cut the second cardboard tube to 2" (5.1 cm) long.

9. Cover one end of this short piece with transparent tape, so the sticky side faces inside the tube.

10. Fill the tube halfway full with craft jewels and/or beads. Some of the jewels should stick to the tape and some will flow free. This will make for better viewing.

11. Cover the open end of the 2" (5.1 cm) tube with plastic wrap, then secure with clear tape.

12. Tape the 2" (5.1 cm) tube to the base of the longer tube to create kaleidoscope.

13. Decorate kaleidoscope with additional construction paper or however you wish.

14. For the best viewing, point the base of your kaleidoscope to the sky to let light come through the jewel chamber.

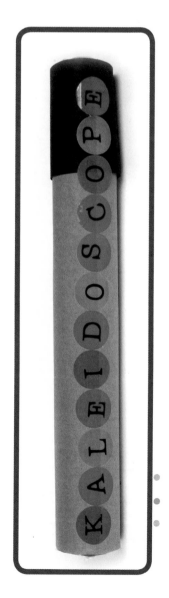

Wind Chime

What you need:

- Cardboard toilet paper tube
- Construction paper
- Cool-temperature glue gun/glue sticks
- Heavy bead, crystal, or disc
- Length of cording
- Markers, stickers or other embellishments
- Metal chimes
- Wooden dowel cut to length of circumference of tube

Instructions

1. Dab a tiny bit of glue on each end of the dowel and insert horizontally into the top of the tube so that it fits snugly.

2. Cover tube with construction paper and decorate with markers, stickers, or any other embellishments.

3. Hang metal chimes from dowel so that they are hidden inside the tube.

4. Tie length of cording to the dowel so that it hangs through the tube, then tie bead, crystal, or disc.

5. Tie another length of cording to hang the wind chime from.

6. Hang chime in a doorway or open window to let the breeze make music for you.

Note: Wind chime is not waterproof, so it is not recommended that you hang outside.

Butterflies

What you need:

- Cardboard toilet paper tube
- Craft glue
- Foam sheets or construction paper
- Markers
- Paint
- Paintbrushes
- Pencil
- Pipe cleaners
- Scissors
- Yarn or plastic string, 8–12 yards (7.32–10.97 m)
- Butterfly stencil (optional)

Instructions

1. Draw or trace a butterfly on a foam sheet or piece of construction paper. *Note: Leave room in the center for the cardboard tube body to be placed.* Cut butterfly out.

2. Paint the cardboard tube and allow to dry.

3. Decorate butterfly with construction paper embellishments or markers, as desired.

4. Glue the cardboard tube up the center of the butterfly as shown in photograph. Curve the wings of the butterfly up over the sides of the tube.

5. Using the point of your scissors or the sharp metal tip of the pipe cleaner, poke a small hole in the top center of the cardboard tube.

6. Cut a pipe cleaner in half and poke it through the hole. Twist the ends of the pipe cleaner to create antennae.

7. Decorate the body of your butterfly as desired.

8. Cut two pieces of string, 4–6 yards (3.66-5.49 m) each. Thread string through body of the butterfly.

Sunflower Vase

Instructions

1. Clean the inside of the potato chip can.

2. Glue green construction paper around the can to make the vase.

3. Use a pencil to trace your hand 6–8 times onto yellow construction paper. *Note: You might want to have a grown-up help you.*

4. Cut out the handprints, then glue them onto the paper plate as shown to make sunflower.

5. Bend black pipe cleaner into a circle and glue to center of sunflower. Glue seeds inside pipe cleaner circle.

6. Twist pipe cleaner around the stick, leaving enough room at the top to tape or glue the sunflower.

7. Tape or glue sunflower to the stick, then place in flower vase.

8. Surround the base of the stick with newspaper or tissue paper so the flower stands up tall.

9. Tie ribbon around the top of the vase.

What you need:

- Cylindrical potato chip can
- Construction paper: green and yellow
- Craft glue
- Green and black pipe cleaners
- Newspaper or tissue paper
- Pencil
- Ribbon
- Scissors
- Small, plain paper plate
- Stick, without leaves
- Sunflower seeds, with shells
- Transparent tape

Picture Frames

Instructions

1. Trim two pieces of cardboard or foam sheets to 4½" x 6" (11.4 cm x 15.2 cm).

2. Cut a 3½" x 5" (8.9 cm x 12.7 cm) rectangle from the center of one of the sheets. The outside portion that remains will act as the front of your frame.

3. Cut the cardboard toilet paper tube Lengthwise in half 2 times, so that you have 4 strips.

4. Color the strips with the brown marker, using small, alternating marks to create the look of logs.

5. Glue camping picture to the middle of the full sheet of cardboard or foam sheet.

6. Place the second sheet of cardboard or foam over the first, so that the hole frames the picture. Glue into place.

7. Line up and adhere toilet paper tube "logs" on the edges of the frame to create the look of a wood frame.

8. Trim any overhanging edges.

9. Decorate your frame with stickers or other embellishments, as desired.

10. Glue magnetic strips to the back of your frame.

11. Give your frame to someone as a gift, or stick it right on your fridge to enjoy!

To make a very simple frame for your favorite pictures, stack several pieces of cardboard together placing pieces of double-stick tape between each layer. Wrap each stack like you would a package with wrapping paper only use scrapbook papers. Attach your picture on the front with double-stick tape. Add stickers, sign and date the back, and you have the perfect gift for Mom and Dad or something new to hang in your room.

What you need:

- Cardboard toilet paper tube
- Cardboard or foam sheet
- 3½" x 5" (8.9 cm x 12.7 cm) camping picture
- Brown marker
- Craft glue
- Embellishments: miniature toys, stickers, etc.
- Ruler
- Scissors
- Two 3" (7.6 cm) magnetic strips

Napkin Rings

Instructions

1. Cut cardboard tube to the width you want your napkin rings to be.

2. Paint tube with glue and cover with seeds in any design you desire.

Optional: Some other options for decorating napkin rings are to wrap the tubes with raffia or ribbon or cover tubes with paper and stickers. You can also spell names for each of your guests.

What you need:

- Cardboard wrapping paper tube
- Colored or decorative paper
- Cool-temperature glue gun/glue sticks
- Double-stick tape
- Ribbon
- Scissors
- Seeds
- Alphabet stickers or other alphabet embellishments (optional)

Rain Stick

Instructions

1. Cut a sheet of aluminum foil to 3 times the length of your cardboard tube.

2. Fold the long edge of the foil over and over, squeezing it into a long strip.

3. Coil the foil into a spring, then push into the cardboard tube so that it reaches from one end to the other.

4. Insert 1 end cap and glue into place. If you do not have end caps, you can make them by cutting 2 cardboard discs to the circumference of the tube.

5. Glue construction paper around the tube.

6. Pour beans or rice into the tube, making sure it's not too heavy.

7. Once you are satisfied with the sound, seal the other end of the tube with the second end cap or cardboard circle.

8. Decorate rain stick as desired with markers, paint, or other embellishments.

What you need:

- Cardboard mailing tube or paper towel tube
- ½ cup (120 ml) dried beans or rice
- Aluminum foil
- Construction paper
- Craft glue
- Mailing tube end caps or cardboard
- Paint, markers, or other desired embellishments
- Scissors

Totem poles are monuments that tell stories. You can create your very own totem pole to tell stories about your family, your favorite animals, or anything else you wish. Let your imagination run wild!

Totem Pole

What you need:
- Cardboard paper towel tube or mailing tube
- 2 wooden craft sticks
- Construction paper
- Craft glue
- Crayons, paint, or markers
- Feathers or other embellishments
- Ruler
- Scissors

Instructions

1. Cut a piece of construction paper to fit around the cardboard tube.

2. Draw lines every 2"–4" (5.1 cm–10.2 cm) down the length of the construction paper, depending on how large you want your decorative pictures.

3. Decorate each section of your paper to tell your totem pole story.

4. Glue the construction paper around the tube.

5. Cut a pair of wings (or ask a grown-up to help you) from a sheet of construction paper and glue to the back of the totem pole.

6. Glue the craft sticks to the back of the wings to make them sturdier. Make sure to glue them so that they can't be seen from the front.

7. Finish your totem pole with feathers or any other embellishments you choose.

Spiral Book

What you need:

- Smooth cardboard mat
- Colored or decorative paper
- Double-stick tape
- Ruler
- Scissors
- Spiral binding
- Stickers or other embellishments

Instructions

1. Cut 2 sheets of cardboard to the size you want your book to be.

2. Use double-stick tape to cover cardboard with paper, then embellish with stickers or any other details that you like. *Note: Make sure to cover the entire piece of cardboard, so that both the inside and outside covers are decorated.*

3. Cut as many sheets of paper as you would like to go inside the notebook to ¼" (0.6 cm) smaller than the covers. *Note: Measurements should be ¼" (0.6 cm) smaller on all sides.*

4. Bind the book with spiral binding. If you do not have a spiral binding system at home, your local copy center can do it for you very cheaply.

Fold-Up Book

What you need:

- Smooth cardboard mat
- Colored or decorative paper
- Craft glue
- Double-stick tape
- Map
- Ribbon
- Scissors

Instructions

1. Cut 2 cardboard sheets to the size you want your book to be.

2. Use double-stick tape to cover cardboard with map.

3. Cut a piece of paper so that it is about double the height of the book cover.

4. Fold paper into an accordion. Double-stick tape first and last page of accordion to front and back covers of books.

5. Glue a ribbon to the inside center of both covers and use as a tie to keep your book shut!

Instructions

1. Cut 2 pieces of cardboard to the size you want your book to be.

2. Cut 1 piece of cardboard to the same height as the front and back covers, but only 2"–3" (5.1–7.6 cm) wide. This will be the book's spine.

3. Measure the width of the cardboard cover, then multiply by 4. Add the width of the spine to this number. Add about 1" (2.5 cm) to this number. *Note: Ask a grown-up to help you with the math if you have not yet learned your multiplication tables or don't have a calculator handy.*

4. For the cover, cut a sheet of paper to the height of the book covers and the width that you just figured out by multiplying and adding.

5. Lay front cover, spine, and back cover in the very center of the very wide sheet of paper, with about ¼" (0.6 cm) between them. This extra space between the spine and covers will allow you to close the book once the paper is stuck to the cardboard.

6. Use double-stick tape to adhere paper to covers and spine, smoothing out wrinkles as you go.

7. Cut as many pieces of paper as you would like to go inside your book, to about ¼" (0.6 cm) smaller than the covers.

8. Stack papers inside cover, or take to your local copy store to have them apply adhesive so you can tear the pages off one at a time.

Square Book

What you need:

- Smooth cardboard mat
- Colored or decorative paper
- Double-stick tape
- Ruler
- Scissors

Guitar

Instructions

1. Measure a 6" long (15.2 cm) oval on the lid of the shoebox and carefully cut out, or ask an adult to help you. *Note: If you are using a tissue box, this will not be necessary, as the hole is already cut out for you.*

2. Cover the box with construction paper.

3. Using the end of the cardboard tube as your guide, trace and cut a hole in the end of the box.

4. Insert the cardboard tube all the way into the box, pushing it down as far as it will go.

5. Add a bit of glue to the hole in the end of the cardboard box to secure the cardboard tube into place.

6. Decorate guitar with additional construction paper embellishments or paint, as desired.

7. Tape the string or rubber band to the base of the guitar and pull up the front of the tube. If you are using a rubber band, remember to cut it so that it is one long string instead of circular.

8. Secure the string at the top of the tube with tape.

What you need:

- Cardboard gift wrap tube
- Construction paper
- Pencil
- Plastic string or long rubber band
- Ruler
- Scissors
- Shoebox or facial tissue box
- Transparent tape
- White glue
- Acrylic paint and paintbrush (optional)

Instructions

1. Wrap cardboard tube with paper and adhere with double-stick tape.

2. Wrap one length of ribbon around each bobbin, then secure with a dab of glue.

3. Embellish package as desired.

4. Cut paper into circles to cover the top and bottom of ribbon bobbins and secure with double-stick tape.

5. Glue or double-stick tape the bobbins to the top and base of the tube.

6. Insert musical gift, attach gift tag, and give your gift to the most musical person you know!

Note: Ideas for musical gifts can come right from this book! Make a special maraca, guitar, or kazoo to fit your gift box!

What you need:

- Cardboard tube
- 2 cardboard ribbon bobbins
- Colored paper or cardstock
- Cool-temperature glue gun/glue sticks
- Double-stick tape
- Embellishments such as rhinestones, stickers, or anything you like!
- Gift tag
- Musical gift to fit box
- Ribbon
- Scissors

Square Box

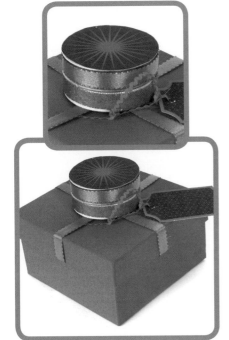

Instructions

1. Wrap one length of ribbon around each bobbin, then secure with a dab of glue.

2. Wrap package with ribbon as shown.

3. Cut paper into circles to cover the top and bottom of ribbon bobbins and secure with double-stick tape.

4. Glue or double-stick tape the bobbins to the top of the package in a fancy arrangement.

5. Insert musical gift, attach gift tag, and give your gift to the most musical person you know!

What you need:

- 2 cardboard ribbon bobbins
- Colored paper or cardstock
- Cool-temperature glue gun/glue sticks
- Double-stick tape
- Gift tag
- Musical gift to fit box
- Ribbon
  Scissors
- Square gift box

Kazoo

Sound waves will vibrate the wax paper on your kazoo and make musical sounds!

Instructions

1. *Note: If using paper towel roll, cut in half before using.* Paint cardboard tube, if desired, and allow to dry.

2. Use compass or circle template and pencil to trace a 6" (15.2 cm) circle onto wax paper, then cut out.

3. Place wax paper over one end of the cardboard tube, securing in place with rubber band.

4. Decorate kazoo with stickers or other embellishments.

5. To use your kazoo, make loud tooting sounds into the open end.

What you need:

- Cardboard toilet paper or paper towel tube
- Compass or 6" (15.2 cm) circle template
- Pencil
- Rubber band
- Scissors
- Stickers or other embellishments
- Wax paper
- Acrylic paint and paintbrush (optional)

Maraca

What you need:
- Cardboard mailing tube with end caps or paper towel tube with cardboard cut to fit ends
- ½ cup (120 ml) dried rice
- 2 wooden craft sticks
- Craft glue
- Markers, patterned paper, stickers (optional)

Instructions

1. Glue the top half of one craft stick inside the cardboard tube, making sure the bottom half remains outside the tube.

2. Glue the top half of the second craft stick to the outside of the cardboard tube, making sure it is lined up with the first stick.

3. Glue the ends of the sticks that are outside the tube firmly together and allow to dry. This will be your maraca handle.

4. Insert one end cap and glue into place. If you do not have end caps, you can make them by cutting two cardboard discs to the circumference of the tube.

5. Pour rice into the tube, then glue the second end cap into place. *Note: The craft stick on the inside of the tube might make this a tighter fit than the first end cap.*

6. Decorate the outside of the tube as desired with markers, patterned paper, stickers, or other desired embellishments.

Check Box Camera

Instructions

1. Cover outside of the check box with construction paper and tape into place.

2. Cut toilet paper tube to 3" (7.6 cm) long.

3. Paint the toilet paper tube. Let dry.

4. Using the toilet paper tube as your guide, trace a circle in the center of the check box, then cut it out with craft knife.

5. Slide the toilet paper tube into the circle cut from the check box, making sure most of it is sticking out.

6. Cut a small square of foil and tape to the upper, right-hand corner of the check box to create the flash. *Note: If you have chosen to use another embellishment instead of the foil, tape this to the upper, right-hand corner of the check box.*

7. Tape small viewfinder-like embellishment next to the flash.

8. Using markers or construction paper, create other camera buttons and features as desired.

What you need:

- Cardboard toilet paper tube
- Acrylic paint
- Check box
- Construction paper
- Craft knife
- Double-stick tape
- Foil or other shiny embellishment
- Markers
- Paintbrush
- Pencil
- Scissors
- Small, viewfinder-like embellishment
- Transparent tape

What you need:

- 2 cardboard toilet paper tubes
- Construction paper: black and green
- Craft glue
- Hole punch
- Scissors
- String or yarn

Binoculars

Instructions

1. Cut the sheet of green construction paper in half lengthwise.

2. Glue the two halves of the construction paper to the 2 cardboard tubes.

3. Cut a long, thin strip [about 1" (2.5 cm)] of black construction paper and cut in half.

4. Glue each strip to the bottom of each cardboard tube.

5. Glue the 2 tubes together.

6. Punch a small hole in either side of the top half of the binoculars.

7. Carefully make sure the string will be long enough to slip the binoculars easily over your head, then tie the ends of the string through the holes.

8. Cut a piece of black construction paper to about 2" x 3" (5.1 cm x 7.6 cm).

9. Roll this piece of construction paper into a small tube and glue to the top of the binoculars to create the focus dial.

Space Shuttle

Instructions

1. Paint the cardboard tube white and allow to dry.

2. Lay the tube on the foam sheet and draw the wings of the shuttle. Leave enough space in the center of the wings for the tube to rest. Cut out wings. You might feel more comfortable asking a grown-up to help you.

3. Draw a triangular tail wing on the foam sheet and cut out.

4. Glue the cardboard tube to the center of the shuttle wings, then add the tail wing as shown in photograph.

5. Insert the foam ball into the end of the tube, then glue into place to create the nose of the shuttle.

6. Use the black marker to draw windows in the nose of the shuttle. Glue embellishments to wings.

What you need:

- Cardboard paper towel tube
- 1½" (3.8 cm) foam ball Black marker
- Craft glue
- Embellishments or stickers
- Paintbrush
- Pencil
- Scissors
- White craft paint
- White foam sheet

Candy Favors

What you need:

- Cardboard paper towel tubes
- 2 pieces of cardboard per rocket, cut to fit holes in tube
- Construction paper
- Candy or small party favors
- Cool-temperature glue gun/ glue sticks
- Double-stick tape
- Markers
- Scissors
- Stickers

Instructions

1. Cut a piece of construction paper to the length and 1½ times the circumference of the tube.

2. Center the tube on the paper. Tape 1 edge of the paper onto the cylindrical portion of the tube.

3. Roll the tube tightly onto the paper securing with double-stick tape at the end of the paper.

4. Cut 4 circles of construction paper to cover both sides of the cardboard circles. Attach paper to cardboard with double-stick tape.

5. Put a ring of glue from the glue gun around the edge of 1 circle and attach to bottom of tube.

6. Cut 4 triangles to make launch pad stabilizers for rocket. Attach to rocket sides with thin strip of glue from glue gun.

7. Cut a circle, then cut a pie wedge from the circle, tape ends of cut circle to make rocket nose.

8. Fill tube with candy or party favors.

9. Attach second covered cardboard circle to top of tube by taping over the circle and onto the tube.

10. Cover top circle with rocket nose.

Rocket

Instructions

1. Wrap construction paper around cardboard tube, then tape or glue into place.

2. Cut 4 slits at one end of the tube. Each slit should be about 2½" (6.4 cm) long, and each pair should be placed directly opposite each other.

3. Cut two triangles that are roughly 4" (10.2 cm) tall with a 5" (12.7 cm) base.

4. Cut a slit in the first triangle to the center of the triangle. Cut in a slit in the second triangle from the center bottom of the triangle to the center.

5. Slip the first triangle (with the slit cut from the bottom to the center) into two of the slits cut into the cardboard tube. Slip the second triangle into the remaining two slits, maneuvering it to sit in the first triangle, so the points line up as shown in photograph.

6. Trace 4" (10.2 cm) circle onto construction paper, then cut out. Cut a slit from one outer edge to the center.

7. Roll circle into a cone shape, taping or gluing into place.

8. Tape cone to the top of the rocket.

9. Decorate with stickers, markers, or crayons.

What you need:

- Cardboard paper towel tube
- Compass or 4" (10.2 cm) circle template
- Construction paper
- Craft glue
- Pencil, markers, or crayons
- Ruler
- Scissors
- Transparent tape
- Stickers (optional)

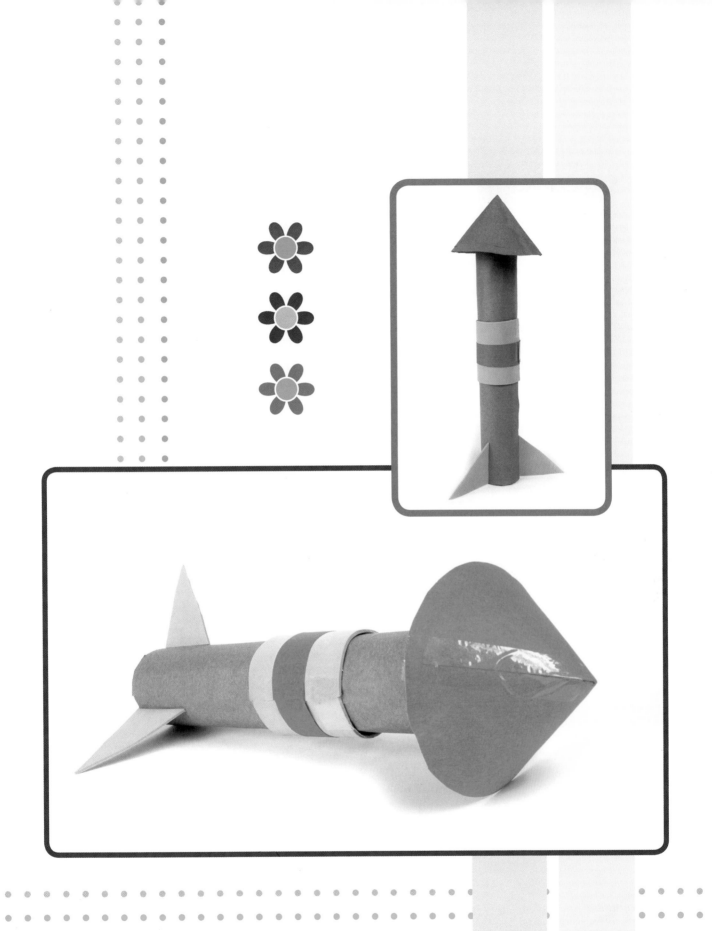

EASY FUN PROJECTS WITH
Craft Sticks

Marsey & Madeline Iverson

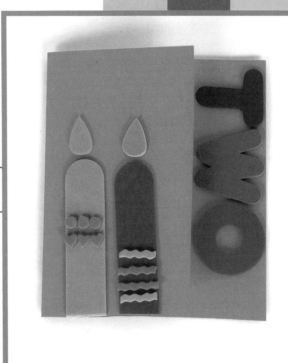

Easy Fun Projects with Craft Sticks

© 2007 by
Mud Puddle Books, Inc.
54 W. 21st Street
Suite 601
New York, NY 10010
info@mudpuddlebooks.com

ISBN: 978-1-60311-119-5

Printed in China

Table of Contents

INTRODUCTION

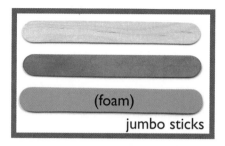

Craft sticks are great for lots of things. You can make gifts, games, picture frames, Christmas ornaments, small animals, or almost anything else that you want from them. They can be painted, glued together, and decorated with anything from yarn to rhinestones. Best of all, they are easy to create with and inexpensive to buy.

Craft sticks are generally made from wood. They come in a variety of sizes and colors, and they can be purchased at your local craft or hobby store. Craft sticks made from "craft foam" are also available for purchase, which come in very bright colors and are flexible— they can be bent into any shape that you wish.

When working with craft sticks, you can use water-based craft paint, white glue or a cool-temperature glue gun, and scissors to cut the sticks to a size you need. You may need an adult to help with cutting the sticks or using the glue gun.

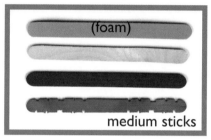

(foam)

jumbo sticks

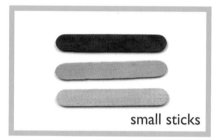

(foam)

medium sticks

small sticks

Hints for Working with Craft Sticks

Cutting

1 Draw a pencil line to help make your cut straight. Put the blade of an old, but sharp, pair of scissors on your line. Close the scissors firmly and cut a small bit at a time. Keep the hand holding the craft stick as close to the cutting line as is safe. This will help to keep the craft stick from splintering.

2 If cutting proves difficult, ask a grown-up for help! *Note: Don't pull or rip, or your end will be very jagged. Even if you cut carefully, your end will be a little jagged. Smooth it out by rubbing it against a piece of sandpaper.*

Gluing with a Glue Gun

1 Always ask a grown-up to help you with your cool-temperature glue gun.

2 When you plug in your cool-temperature glue gun, it will take a few minutes to heat up. Unplug the gun whenever you walk away from your project area.

3 Use an old cooking pot or other heat-proof receptacle to hold the glue gun when you aren't using it. This will prevent the gun from burning surfaces or dripping glue.

4 The metal tip may be hot. You might get burned if you touch it, so don't touch it!

5 The glue sets very quickly—within a few seconds. Try to glue just one small section at a time, so you have time to get the piece in the right place before the glue sets.

6 Don't use a bigger blob of glue than you need, but don't use too little, or the areas to be joined won't hold.

7 Use a plastic knife to wipe off extra glue before it sets. If the glue has already set, the hot tip of the glue gun will melt it again.

Painting

1 You can either paint all of your craft sticks before you begin your project or you can paint the project after it is completed. If you have a number of sticks that are going to be the same color, then it may be easier to paint them beforehand. Otherwise, you may want to see what the project looks like before you decide on the colors.

2 Acrylic craft paint is inexpensive, comes in many colors, is non-toxic, fairly (but not completely) washable, and covers well.

3 You may need to apply at least two coats of paint if you want solid, opaque coverage.

4 Try to make each coat of paint thin and even. Avoid the temptation to do one thick coat instead of two thin ones—one coat of thick paint takes forever to dry and looks amateurish.

Picture Frames

What you need:

- 4 craft sticks for each frame
- Cool-temperature glue gun/glue sticks
- Photograph
- Embellishments (optional)
- Ribbon (optional)

Instructions

1. Put a dab of glue on both ends of 2 sticks. Glue these to the top of 2 additional sticks.

2. Put a tiny bit of glue on the photograph side of each corner of the photograph and place it behind frame window.

   Optional: Glue a ribbon to 2 corners at the back of the frame for hanging, or add embellishments for a designer touch.

Hair Accessories Organizers

Bright Pink

What you need:

- 4 craft sticks
- Cool-temperature glue gun/glue sticks
- Flat rhinestones
- Netting
- Ribbon

Note: There are a variety of nettings available for purchase at your local craft store.

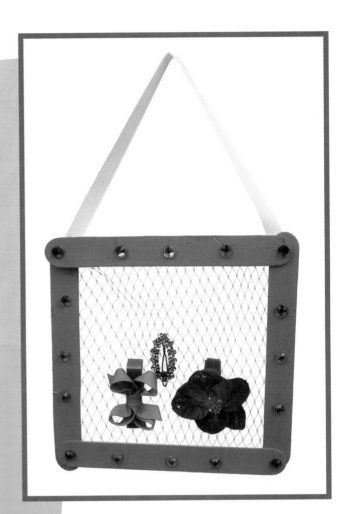

Instructions

1. Put a dab of glue on both ends of 2 sticks. Glue these to the top of 2 additional sticks.

2. Place a line of glue along the backside of 1 craft stick, then adhere netting. Be careful not to touch the glue. Repeat with other 3 sides.

3. Put glue on both ends of the ribbon and press to the back of 2 corners of frame to create hanger.

4. Using glue gun, stick rhinestones into place one at a time.

5. Use to hang barrettes or other hair accessories.

Pastel Pink

To make this organizer, use ribbon in place of netting.

Notepad Holder

What you need:

- 3 large craft sticks
- 17 medium-sized craft sticks
- 2 colors paint
- Cool-temperature glue gun/glue sticks
- Paintbrushes
- Self-adhesive notepad
- Embellishments (optional)
- Wooden or foam letters (optional)

Instructions

1. Paint 1 side of sticks 1 color. Let dry.

2. Paint the other side of the sticks a second color. Let dry.

3. Take 1 medium craft stick and glue the ends of 11 craft sticks to it.

4. Glue another stick along the bottom edge of the 11 craft sticks. This will be the base of your holder.

5. Stack and glue 2 sticks together and glue to the side of the 11 flat sticks to create a wall. Repeat on other side.

6. Glue 1 large craft stick to the top end of the holder, so that it lies perpendicularly to the side walls.

7. Lie 2 large craft sticks across the top of the side walls and glue.

Optional: Write your name with wooden or foam letters at the top of the holder. Decorate with glitter, rhinestones, or other embellishments. Or, just leave your holder plain.

8. Insert notepad and write yourself a note!

Desktop Organizer

What you need:

- Craft sticks: colored or painted
- Cool-temperature glue gun/glue sticks
- Foam dots
- Tin can

Instructions

1. Paint craft sticks, if necessary, and let dry.
2. Glue sticks to the side of can.
3. Adhere foam dots.
4. Fill can with pencils, pens, rulers, scissors, and anything else you would like to store there!

What you need:

- Craft sticks
- Decorated can or glass jar
- Medium craft sticks
- Ultra-fine tip markers
- Variety of paint colors

Wish Sticks

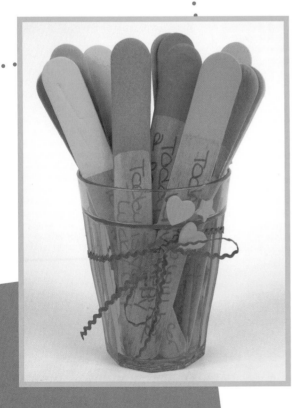

Instructions

1. Dip each stick—about a quarter of the way down—into various colors of paint. Lie across the top of the jar to let dry—do not let the wet paint sit directly on a surface.
2. Write a different wish on each stick.
3. Place sticks in a decorated can or a pretty glass jar.
4. Place your wish sticks by your bed, in the kitchen, or anywhere you want to. Each day, pull a wish stick from the can.
5. Place your wishes back into the can and see if you draw the same wish more than one day in a row!

Woven Trivet

What you need:

- 11 craft sticks
- 3 different kinds of ribbon
- Cool-temperature glue gun/glue sticks

Instructions

1. Take 1 craft stick and glue the ends of 7 craft sticks to it.

2. Fold first ribbon over the seventh craft stick and glue to back side. Begin weaving ribbon over-and-under the 7 craft sticks. Fold ribbon over first craft stick and glue to back side.

3. Glue second ribbon to the back side of the first craft stick, then weave over-and-under sticks. Glue to back side of last craft stick. Make sure that you weave the ribbons over alternating craft sticks.

4. Continue weaving 3 ribbons in this order, until the entire length of the sticks are woven. *Note: You can alternate ribbons in any design that you want.*

5. Glue 1 craft stick under all 7 on opposite end.

FROG PARTY

What you need:

- 1 foam craft stick for each cup
- 1 foam craft stick for each letter of birthday person's name
- 2 foam craft sticks
- 2 large plates *Note: The cake plate will be stronger if you use plastic plates and not paper*
- Cool-temperature glue gun/ glue sticks
- Embellishments: plastic animals or other party themed
- Foam letters to spell birthday person's name
- Matching bowl
- Matching cups
- Party favors

Cake Plate

Instructions

1. Fill cups with something heavy to weight the plate.
2. Glue first plate to top of first cup.
3. Glue second cup to top of first plate.
4. Glue second plate to top of second cup.
5. Glue third cup to top of second plate.
6. Glue bowl to top of third cup.
7. Glue foam craft sticks to side of first plate to act as handles.
8. Glue foam letters to foam craft sticks.
9. Embellish bowl by gluing plastic animals around the rim and then filling with name and embellishments that match your party theme!

Party Favors
Instructions

1. Glue ribbon to inside edges of cups to form handles.
2. Decorate cups.
3. Fill with favors.
4. Decorate the cake table with these wonderful party favors. But be careful—everyone will want more than one!

Flowers in a Row

What you need:

- Craft sticks: medium and small
- Cool-temperature glue gun/glue sticks
- Paint
- Paintbrushes
- Embellishments (optional)
- Terra cotta flower pot or egg carton (optional)

Instructions

1 Glue 2 small sticks to the base of 1 medium stick at 45° angles to create stem and leaves.

2 Use small craft sticks to create desired flower shape and glue together.

3 Paint flower, stem, and leaves. Let dry.

4 Glue on embellishments as desired.

5 "Plant" in an egg carton, in miniature individual flower pots, or put in the top of a cupcake.

Wreath

What you need:

- 7 large craft sticks
- 12 small, green, spoon-shaped craft sticks
- Cool-temperature glue gun/glue sticks
- Embellishments, such as buttons, glitter, pipe cleaners, pom-poms, etc.
- Foam or cardstock flowers
- Ribbon, long enough to tie a bow

Instructions

1 Place a dab of glue on the ends of 1 large stick, then glue to the ends of 2 more large sticks.

2 Continue in this manner until you have a wreath shape.

3 In center of all but bottom stick, glue 2 green spoon-shaped sticks in a criss-cross pattern.

4 Glue a foam or cardstock flower to the top of each set of crossed sticks.

5 Embellish each flower with buttons, rhinestones, pom-poms, glitter, pipe cleaners, or whatever you choose.

6 Tie ribbon in a bow at the bottom of the wreath.

7 Hang on the door of your room, in the kitchen, or give as a gift.

Flowers Are the Sweetest Things...

What you need:

- 3 medium foam craft sticks
- 3 foam flowers
- Blank card
- Cool-temperature glue gun/glue sticks
- Fine-tip felt marker

Instructions

1. Glue foam craft sticks and foam flowers to front of card.

2. Write "Flowers are the sweetest thing... because they're just like you!" or other desired message inside the card.

Spring Basket

What you need:

- 2 foam craft sticks
- Candy
- Cool-temperature glue gun/glue sticks
- Plastic cup
- Scissors

Instructions

1. Glue 1 craft stick around rim of cup, trimming ends if necessary.

2. Glue foam craft stick handle over first craft stick.

3. Fill basket with candy and give to someone special!

14

Flowers

What you need: (for 1 flower)

- 1 notched craft stick
- 2 cardstock or foam flower shapes
- Craft knife
- Gum drop

Instructions

1. Cut slit in center of both flowers and slide over craft stick.

2. Place gum drop on stick end as flower center.

3. Put in a vase, use as a decoration on a cupcake, or put it on your desk in your pencil holder!

Place Cards

What you need: (for 1 place card)

- Craft stick
- Cool-temperature glue gun/glue sticks
- Fine-tip felt marker
- Foam, cardstock, or wooden flower
- Paint: green and a variety of colors of choice
- Paintbrushes
- Polystyrene foam ball

Instructions

1. Paint craft stick green. Let dry.
2. Paint foam ball green. Let dry.
3. Write name or desired message on flower center.
4. Glue stick to back of flower.
5. Put stick in foam base.
6. Set place cards on the dinner table to let everyone know where he or she should be sitting.

Sun Catchers

What you need:

- 3 medium notched craft sticks
- Cool-temperature glue gun/glue sticks
- Rhinestones
- Ribbon or string for hanging

Instructions

1. Glue sticks on top of each other to form a star pattern.
2. Glue rhinestones to star one at a time.
3. Hang in a window so the sun will catch and reflect light from your sun catcher.

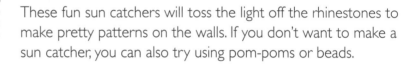

These fun sun catchers will toss the light off the rhinestones to make pretty patterns on the walls. If you don't want to make a sun catcher, you can also try using pom-poms or beads.

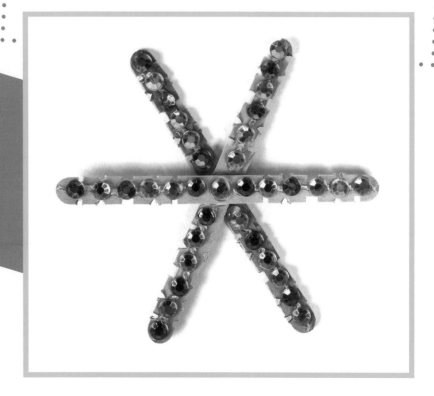

Make It Match

What you need:

- Colored craft sticks
- Cool-temperature glue gun/glue sticks
- Markers or embellishments
- Tin can or cup

Instructions

1. On the end of the first 2 sticks, draw or glue the same design.

2. Repeat with all remaining craft sticks, until you have several sets of craft sticks.

3. Put all of the sticks into the can or cup. Take turns drawing pairs. If your sticks match, you get to keep the pair. If not, put them back. The player with the most pairs at the end of the game wins.

Note: When actually playing the game put sticks object side down into a jar that you cannot see into.

Note: If older children are playing the game, all of the craft sticks should be the same color. If very young children are playing the game, there should be 2 craft sticks of several different colors in order to bring the matching game to their age level.

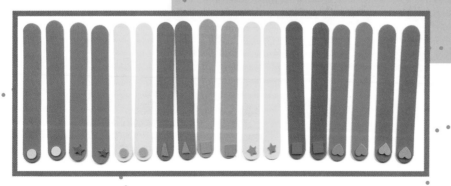

A Puzzle

What you need:

- Jumbo craft sticks
- Craft knife
- Photograph
- White craft glue

Instructions

1. Place enough craft sticks side-by-side so that they are about ½" (1.3 cm) larger on all sides than the picture you have chosen.

2. Paint white glue on the back of the picture and place on top of craft sticks. Gently press the wrinkles out of the picture. Let dry.

3. Turn sticks over and with sharp craft knife and, with the help of a grown-up, slice through the cracks between the craft sticks to cut the paper and separate the sticks.

4. Mix up the puzzle pieces and put it back together.

Tic-Tac-Toe

What you need:

- 4 jumbo craft sticks
- Cool-temperature glue gun/glue sticks
- Foam flowers and squares

Instructions

1. Glue 4 craft sticks into tic-tac-toe board.

2. Practice until you never lose!

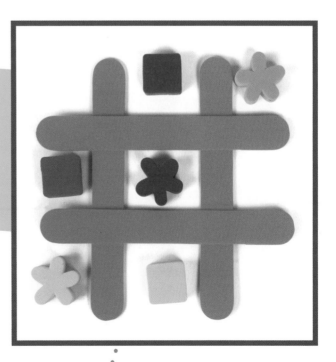

Table & Chair

Note: These projects are intended for older children.

What you need:

- 5 small craft sticks
- 11 jumbo craft sticks

  Cool-temperature glue gun/ glue sticks
- Paint

Instructions

1 Place 4 jumbo sticks on the table so they have a slight space between them. Put a dab of glue on each stick and stick 2 small sticks on top of glue dots. *Note: This will hold your tabletop together.*

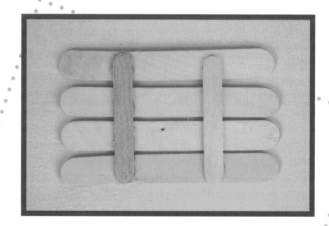

2 Glue 1 jumbo stick on each long side of tabletop and 1 small stick on each end of tabletop.

3 Cut legs desired length, glue legs in place underneath table in each corner. Ask for adult help when cutting.

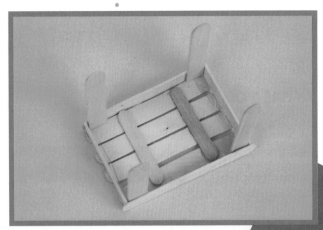

4 Glue jumbo stick in place as table support.

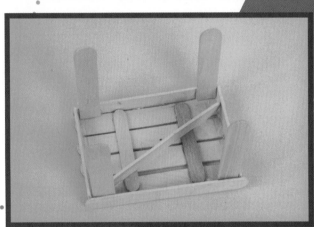

5 Glue small stick in place to resemble drawer.

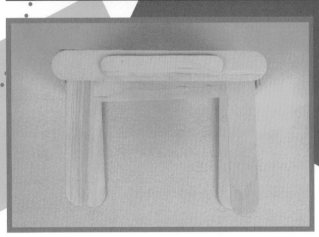

6 Paint table and glue bead for drawer handle.

Chair

What you need:

- 3 jumbo craft sticks
- 11 small craft sticks
- Cool-temperature glue gun/ glue sticks
- Paint
- Paintbrushes

Instructions

1 Front legs of chair: Cut 1 jumbo stick into 2 pieces rounded on 1 end. Ask for adult help when cutting.

2 Put a dot of glue on either end of 1 small craft stick and place on straight end of one stick. Put a dot of glue on second small stick and place slightly below first stick.

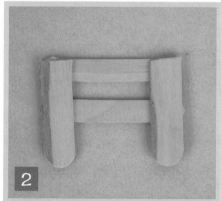

3 Chair back and back legs: Place 2 jumbo sticks next to the 2 sticks in step 2, align rounded bottoms, and repeat step 2.

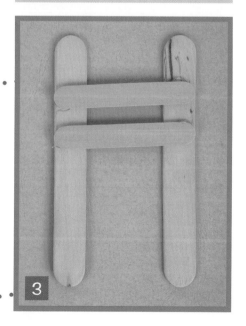

4   Chair seat: Glue 5 small sticks together with a thin thread of glue on one side of each stick.

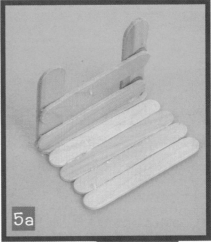

5a

5   Glue the front legs to the front of the seat and the back legs to the back of the seat.

5b

6   Glue 2 small sticks to the underside of the chair as support.

7   Paint chair.

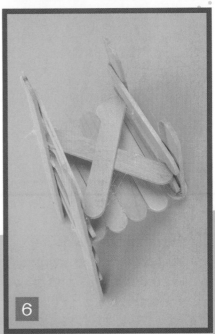

6

Bed

What you need:

- 4 medium craft sticks
- 8 small craft sticks
- 13 jumbo craft sticks
- Cool-temperature glue gun/ glue sticks
  Paint
- Paintbrush

Instructions

1 Footboard – place 1 medium stick on hard surface. Place a jumbo stick on each end of medium stick (do not glue in place). With a dab of glue on the end of 4 small sticks, glue the small sticks to the medium stick, in the space between the 2 jumbo sticks

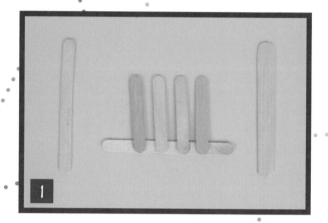

2 Repeat with bottom medium stick.

3 Glue jumbo stick under each end of medium stick.

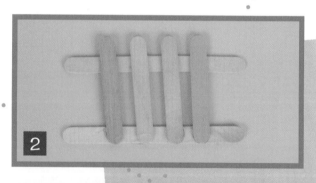

4 Headboard – repeat Steps 1–3 only turn the opposite way so the small sticks are at the top.

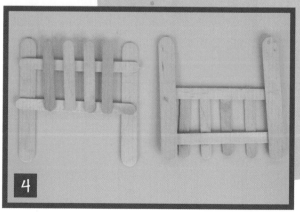

24

5 Bed – Glue 6 jumbo sticks together with a thin thread of glue on each side of stick.

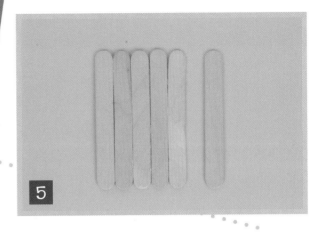

6 Bed support - Turn bed upside down and glue 2 jumbo sticks on each side.

7 Glue footboard to bottom of bed and headboard to top of bed.

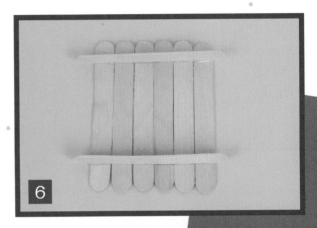

8 Glue one jumbo stick diagonally across bottom of bed for support.

9 Paint.

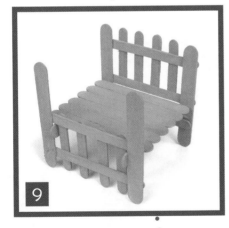

10 Decorate with miniature linens and pillows or cover the bed with roses – you now have your own "bed of roses"!

Horse & Buck Fence

What you need:

- 5 medium craft sticks
- 10 small craft sticks
- Black yarn
- Black felt
- Magic markers: black and brown
- Paintbrush
- Scissors
- String: black and cream
- White glue or cool-temperature glue gun/glue sticks

Instructions

Horse:

1 Use 1 small craft stick as body.

2 Cut medium craft stick to 1½" (3.8 cm) to use as head, and to 1" (2.5 cm) to use as the neck. Ask a grown-up for help with cutting.

3 Glue neck piece of stick to end of the small body stick, then glue head piece to neck. Glue 2 small sticks to each side of body stick for legs.

4 Paint bottom hooves with black magic marker.

5 Paint craft sticks with glue, then wrap legs, body, and head with yarn.

6 Cut two small ears from felt, then glue to head.

7 Cut string for mane and tail. Glue to body.

Fence:

1 Glue sticks together as shown.

2 Create "wood" pattern on sticks using brown magic marker.

3 Tie horse to fence.

Fish

What you need:

- 8 small craft sticks per fish
- 2 paper plates
- Cool-temperature glue gun/glue sticks
- Google eye
- Hole punch
- Paint: 2 colors of choice
- Paper garland
- Ribbon

Instructions for fish

1 Paint 6 craft sticks one color and 2 a different color.

2 Overlap 6 sticks as shown in photo. Remove 1 at a time, add glue, and replace.

3 Glue different color stick across top of 6.

4 Turn fish over and repeat with second different colored stick.

5 Glue google eye and ribbon to fish.

Instructions for mobile

1 Punch groups of 2 holes around the inside of 1 plate.

2 Thread ribbon through and secure. Tie end of ribbon to fish. *Note: to strengthen the holes you can slide a craft stick under the ribbon between the holes on the backside of the plate.*

3 Glue wrong sides of 2 plates together.

4 Glue paper garland between plates.

5 Attach something to top plate to hang mobile from. *Note: We used the fishing pole that came with a child's game.*

6 Hang somewhere you can enjoy the bright colors everyday!

Butterflies

What you need:

- Colored craft sticks
- Cool-temperature glue gun/glue sticks
- Embellishments
- Pipe cleaners
- Scissors
- Scrapbook papers

Instructions:

1 Cut butterfly wings from papers in different sized heart shapes.

2 Glue wings to back of craft stick.

3 Fold pipe cleaner and glue to stick about 1'' (2.5 cm) from the top.

4 Embellish butterfly wings as desired.

5 Put butterfly on top of a special package, hang in the window, pin to your shirt, or do whatever you want with your new butterfly!

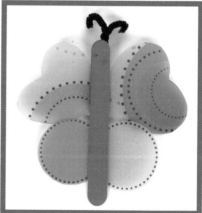

Birds of a Feather

Instructions

1. Paint craft stick and ball. Let dry.
2. Make face on foam flower with foam shapes, google eyes, and/or black marker.
3. Glue to craft stick.
4. Insert stick in front of ball and feathers in back of ball.

What you need: (for 1 bird)

- 1 small craft stick
- 1 polystyrene foam ball with flat side
- Cool-temperature glue gun/glue sticks
- Feathers
- Felt shapes for eyes and nose
- Foam flower shape
- Paint
- Paintbrushes
- Ultra-fine black magic marker

Sailboats

What you need:

- Colored craft sticks
- Crispy rice treat or gum drop
- Foam
- Foam letters and decorations
- Paper plate
- Scissors

Instructions

1. Cut sail shapes from foam, then cut 2 slits in each sail. *Note: you can write your friend's name on the sail or put a cut-out foam initial.*

2. Insert stick between slits.

3. Insert bottom of stick into crispy rice treat or gum drop.

4. Put on a paper plate and serve your friends something new after school.

What you need: (for 1 airplane)

- 2 medium craft sticks
- 4 small craft sticks
- Cool-temperature glue gun/glue sticks
- Magic markers

Instructions

1. Glue 1 medium stick perpendicularly to the other medium stick to create the wings and body.

2. Glue 2 small sticks in an X shape to create the propeller.

3. Glue 1 small stick across the end of the body to create the tail.

4. Cut 1 small stick in half and glue the cut end to tail.

5. Color with markers as desired.

6. Set planes on your desk, hang together in a mobile, or write the name of a friend on the body and give to him or her as a gift.

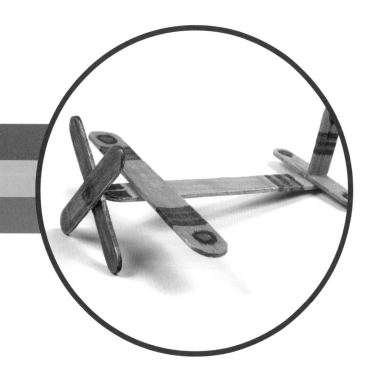

Maddi

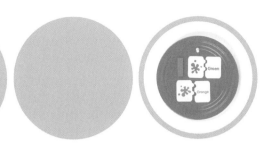

EASY FUN PROJECTS WITH

· ·

Paper Plates & Cups

Jo Packham

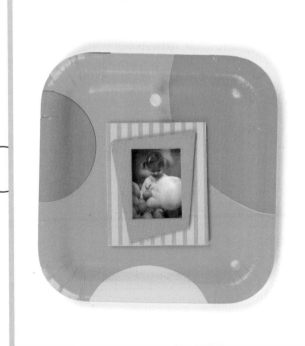

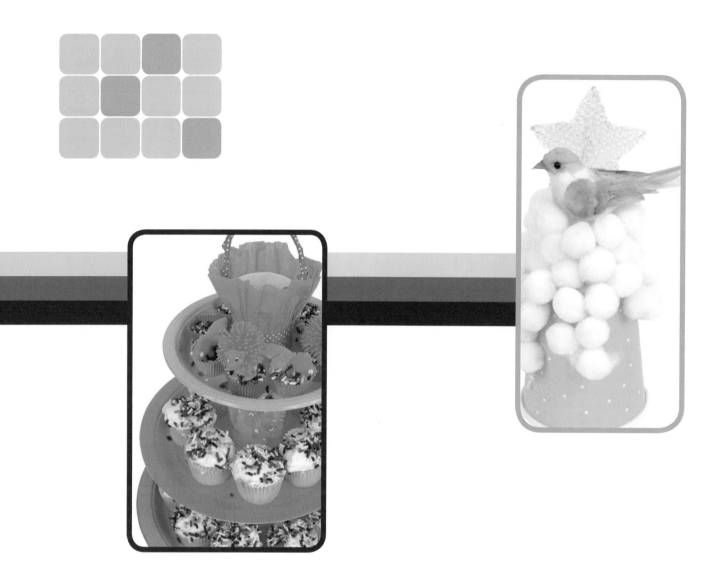

Easy Fun Projects with
Paper Plates & Cups
by Jo Packham

© 2007 by
Mud Puddle Books, Inc.
54 W. 21st Street
Suite 601
New York, NY 10010
info@mudpuddlebooks.com

ISBN: 978-1-60311-117-1

Printed in China

Table of Contents

When you think of paper plates and cups, you probably think of picnics, birthday parties, and other celebrations filled with family and friends. But paper plates and cups are so much fun to make things out of, too! With just a few paper or plastic plates and cups, as well as some glue, embellishments, and some markers, you can create holiday decorations, exciting gifts for your family, and party decorations.

When you are making some of the projects in this book, you might be asked to use a cool-temperature glue gun and/or a pair of scissors. Always make sure to ask a grown-up for help with the glue gun, as it can get hot. You don't want to hurt yourself while making these projects. Additionally, always use care when cutting with scissors. If something seems too difficult for you to cut by yourself, be sure to find someone that can help you.

Finally, remember to be creative and to have fun with the projects! Don't worry if something doesn't turn out perfectly—sometimes the best projects are the ones with small flaws in them. Decorate your room with your creations, show them off on the refrigerator door, or give them to your grandparents, parents, or babysitter to remind them of how great you are!

When creating projects with paper plates and cups you can cut and glue to make new creative pieces or you can simply decorate the plates and cups as is and use them for something unexpected. For example, the plates and cups to the right are a special party presentation for hot chocolate: fill one cup with chocolate mix and the other cups with something wonderful to put in your hot chocolate. It is simple, it is fun, and everyone will be very impressed!

Frosty the Snowman

What you need:

- 1 small paper plate
- 2 large paper plates
- Buttons
- Cool-temperature glue gun/ glue sticks
- Foam embellishments for face

Instructions

1. Overlap the edges of three plates in a vertical line, then glue together.
2. Glue buttons to center of two bottom plates.
3. Glue foam embellishments to face.
4. Hang on a door to welcome guests to a winter holiday party!

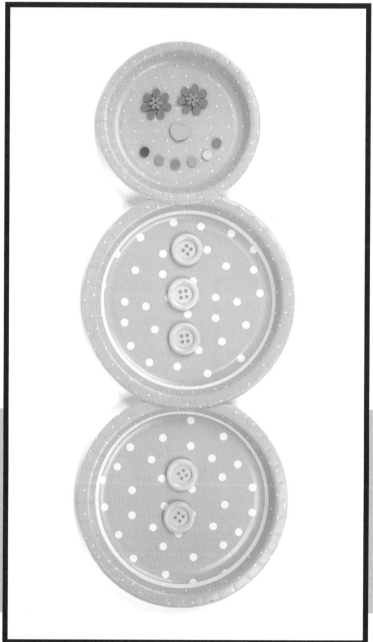

Instructions

1. Decorate cups with desired embellishments.

2. Glue cups to plate.

3. Fill each cup with 1 gift.

4. Surround gift with wrapping materials, making sure the gift is fully hidden and wrapping material sticks out the top of the cup.

5. Tie on gift tag and give to someone very special!

It's a Gift!

What you need:

- 1 large plate
- 4 paper cups
- Cool-temperature glue gun/ glue sticks
- Embellishments
- Gifts to fit paper cups
- Gift tag
- Wrapping materials: curling ribbon, feather boa, shredded paper, tissue paper

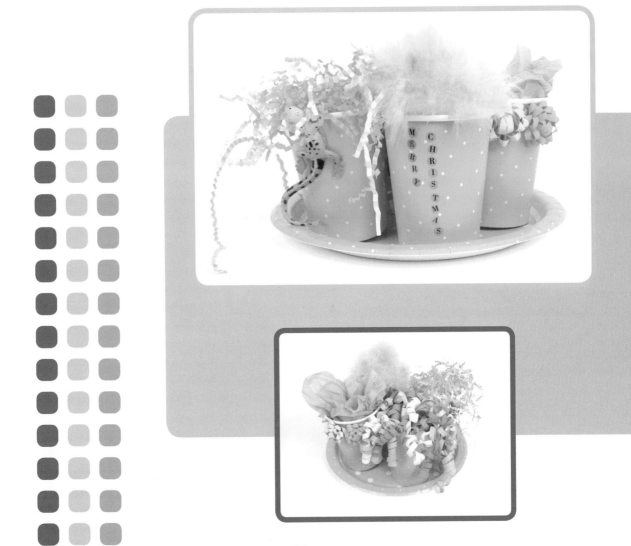

O Christmas Tree, O Christmas Tree

What you need:
- Paper cup
- Cool-temperature glue gun/ glue sticks
- Small, decorative bird
- Small, decorative star
- White pom-poms

Instructions

1. Turn cup upside down and glue pom-poms down the side of cup so that it looks like snow falling.
2. Glue bird on top.
3. Glue star behind bird.
4. Place on the mantel or in the center of the table for your holiday decorating!

Holiday Wreath

Instructions

1. Cut hole in center of paper plate to resemble a wreath.
2. Glue paper garland around edge of plate.
3. Decorate wreath with your favorite embellishments and treasures.
4. Hang on the door to your room or over the fireplace for the holiday season.

For A Princess

What you need:
- Paper cups
- Embellishments
- Fishing line
- Glue dots
- Hole punch
- Scissors
- Royal treats (optional)

Instructions

1 Cut the top of the paper cups with scissors in the shape of crowns.

2 Embellish each crown as desired.

3 Punch a hole in each side of crown and add a fishing line handle.

4 Hang from Christmas tree empty or fill with "royal" treats.

Note: Crowns may also be used as party favors for which you would eliminate the fishing line handle.

Ladybug, Ladybug

What you need:
(for 1 Ladybug)

- 1 large paper plate
- 1 medium paper plate
- 1 pipe cleaner
- 2 large pom-poms
- Cool-temperature glue gun/ glue sticks
- Dots: foam cut-outs, pom-poms, stickers, etc.
- Ribbon
- Scissors

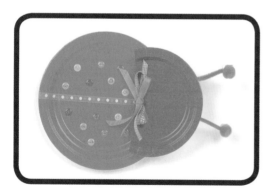

Instructions

1. Cut medium plate to slightly larger than half the original size.

2. Glue ribbon down center of large plate.

3. Glue medium plate to large plate at ridge.

4. Embellish with ladybug "dots".

5. Cut 2 pieces of pipe cleaner, glue to back of medium paper plate, attach 1 pom-pom to each pipe cleaner.

6. Hang wherever you would like to see it most—it will make every day a party day!

Wear Your Party Hat!

Instructions

1 Place hat in middle of plate. On the right side of the hat, punch one hole on the outside edge of the hat, then one hole on the plate inside the hat. Repeat on the left side of hat. *Note: This means the plate will have 4 holes punched into it—2 on the outer edges of the hat and 2 on the inside, where you can't see them.*

2 If your hat does not already have holes in it, punch 2 holes in the hat to line up with holes punched in the plate.

3 Thread ribbon up through right outside hole, through hole in hat, then down through inside hole. Tie a knot under the plate to secure hat to plate, then repeat on left side.

4 Glue garland to rim of plate.

5 Embellish hat with favorite party items.

6 Wrap desired embellishments with pipe cleaners. Stick pipe cleaner in center top of hat.

7 Punch an additional hole on each side of the plate to thread a ribbon through, so you can wear your new party hat!

What you need:

- 1 large plate
- 1 party hat
- Cool-temperature glue gun/ glue sticks
- Embellishments
- Fringed paper garland
- Hole punch
- Pipe cleaners
- Ribbon

It's a Party!

Tiered Cake Plate

Instructions

1. Fill cups with party favors or candy.
2. Glue largest plate to first cup.
3. Glue second cup to top of first plate.
4. Glue medium plate to top of second cup.
5. Glue last cup to top of second plate.
6. Glue smallest plate to top of third cup.
7. Glue chosen centerpiece to top plate.
8. Fill with treats and place in the center of the party table!

What you need:

- 1 large plastic plate
- 1 medium plastic plate
- 1 small plastic plate
- 3 clear plastic glasses
- Centerpiece: party cup, Chinese takeout box, decorated glass, or paper-mache box
- Cool-temperature glue gun/ glue sticks
- Party favors or candy to fill cups *Note: Party favors must be "heavy" to hold plate secure. If they are not, put a rock in the bottom of the cup before you add the favors.*

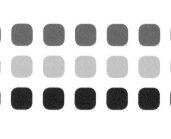

14

Garland

What you need:

- Small plates
- Cool-temperature glue gun/ glue sticks
- Feather boa or ribbon
- Foam embellishments
- Hole punch

Instructions

1. Cut plates in half. *Note: You will need enough plates to make your garland as long as you want it to be.*

2. Embellish plates as desired.

3. Punch holes in both sides of each plate and tie 2 plates together using the boa or a ribbon.

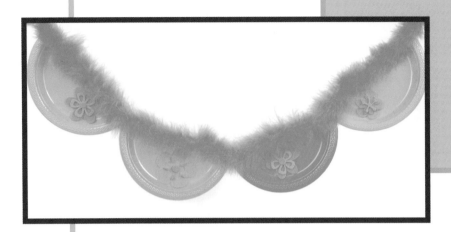

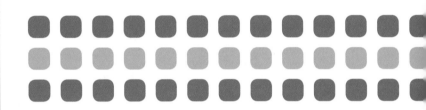

Party Cups

What you need:

- Party cups
- Cool-temperature glue gun/ glue stick
- Embellishments

Instructions

1. Decorate cups with your chosen embellishments.

2. Fill with lemonade and serve!

Welcome To Fairyland

...where everyone
is a princess

What you need:

- Paper plates
- Burgundy magic marker
- Decorative-edged scissors
- Double-stick tape
- Hole punch
- Images cut from old greeting cards
- Ribbon

Instructions

1. Using decorative-edged scissors, cut images the size of the inside circle of the plate from old greeting cards.

2. Adhere images to center of plates with double-stick tape.

3. Write: *Welcome to Fairyland…* on one plate and *…where everyone is a Princess* on a second plate.

4. Punch one hole in the top of each plate and thread ribbon through.

5. Hang from the ceiling over the party table or around your room.

Pizza Man

What you need:

- 1 cup
  1 plate
- Brown paper
  Double-stick tape
- Embellishments
  Markers
- Ruler
  Scissors

Instructions

1. Using ruler and a marker, draw pizza pie lines on your plate.

2. Cut out 1 slice of pizza.

3. Decorate pizza with "pepperoni" circles of brown paper. Draw any additional pizza toppings that you like with markers.

4. Decorate cup with embellishments.

5. Use as table decorations at your next football party!

Party Animals: Soccer, Football, and Baseball Guys

What you need:

- Cups
- Double-stick tape
  Embellishments: sports-themed papers and stickers
- Miniature sports balls

Instructions

1. Embellish cups as desired.
2. To "top" cups off, use miniature balls. *Note: Our sports balls are actually bubble containers, but you can use any type you wish!*

Hairy Party Guys

What you need:
- Paper cups
- Embellishments: foam cutouts, google eyes, etc.
- Glue dots
- Succulent plants or grass

Instructions
1. Make party guy faces on cups with embellishments as desired.
2. Fill cups with dirt and plant succulent plants or grass.
3. Put on your desk or give as a gift, and water occasionally.

Full Speed Ahead!

This race car themed desk set will make a statement in any racing fan's office space! If you can't find the checkered plates and cups, just draw the pattern on yourself—this added touch will make your work extra special!

Paperweight

What you need:

- Black-and-white checkered paper cup
- Race car embellishments
- Sand

Instructions

1. Fill cup with sand.
2. Decorate cup if you want to, and fill with any extra embellishments.
3. Use to keep all your important papers in place!

Memo Boards

What you need:

- Black-and-white checkered paper plates
- Cool-temperature glue gun/ glue sticks
- Corkboard squares or circles to fit bottom of paper plates
- Embellishments
- Thumbtacks

Instructions

1. Glue cork to the back of the paper plates.
2. Glue embellishments where you want them.
3. Hang on wall over desk.
4. Use thumbtacks to pin up important memos, phone numbers, or pictures!

Office Supply Containers

What you need:

- Black-and-white checkered paper cups
- Cool-temperature glue gun/ glue sticks
- Embellishments
- Office supplies: paperclips, rubber bands, etc.

Instructions

1. Embellish cups as desired.
2. Fill with office supplies… except save 1 cup for candy. Everyone needs a treat when they are studying!

Sam's Room

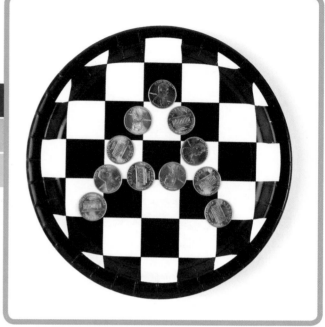

Instructions

1. Spell your name using one paper plate for each letter. *Note: use your imagination when choosing objects to create a letter and when putting the letter on the plate.*

2. Adhere letter to plate with the appropriate adhesive.

3. Attach one piece of Velcro® to the back of each plate and the adjoining piece of Velcro® to the door to your room.

4. Attach plates to Velcro® pieces on the door.

What you need:

- Paper plates
- Adhesives: cool-temperature glue gun/glue sticks, double-stick tape, glue dots
- Embellishments: foam, paper, pennies, rhinestones, stickers, etc.
- Velcro®

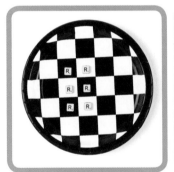

On The Wall

What you need:

- Paper plates
- Cool-temperature glue gun/ glue sticks
- Embellishments: favorite photos, flash cards, plastic fork, ribbon, small wood picture frame, etc.
- Office supplies: post-it notes, pencils, pens, etc.
- Picture hangers

Instructions

1. Adhere different embellishments and office supplies to each plate.

2. Attach picture hanger to back of each plate and to the wall over your desk.

3. Hang plates and use them as individual bulletin boards.

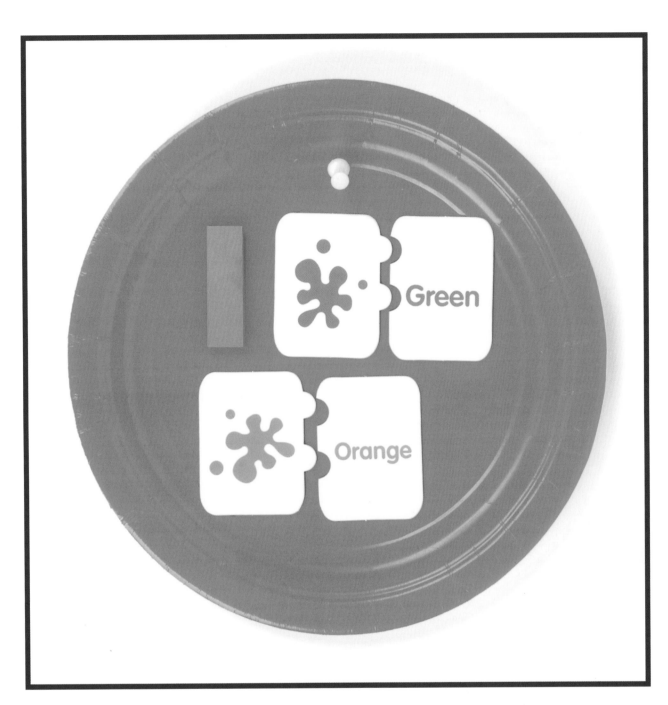

Flower Pockets

What you need:
(for 1 pocket)

- 2 plastic plates
- Cool-temperature glue gun/ glue sticks
- Cupcake liners: different colors, patterns, and sizes
- Embellishments
- Foam sheets
- Hole punch
- Needle and thread
- Mini brads
- Ribbon
- Scissors

Instructions

1. Cut one plate in half.
2. Turn half plate piece over and glue it's rim to rim of whole plate forming a pocket.
3. Punch 2 holes in top of plate and thread ribbon through for hanging. Tie a knot at the top of the ribbon.
4. Make flowers, leaves, and stems (see Instructions on next page).
5. Glue stems to plate, glue flowers to plate over stems, glue leaves under the flowers.
6. Glue embellishments.
7. Hang in your room to make everyday seem like a beautiful spring day!

Flowers:

1. Separate cupcake liners and fold each liner in half.

2. Layer folded liners on top of each other. The more you use, the fuller your flower will be. *Note: Stack liners largest to smallest.*

3. Punch a hole in the middle of the bottom section of stacked liners.

4. Insert brad and secure.

5. Rotate each folded liner so that they overlap and there are no empty spaces.

6. Open and fluff liners so there are no empty spaces in the petals.

Leaves & Stems:

1. Cut stems and leaf shapes from foam sheets.

2. Pinch bottom of leaf together and stitch one small stitch to hold in place.

Pretty in Pink

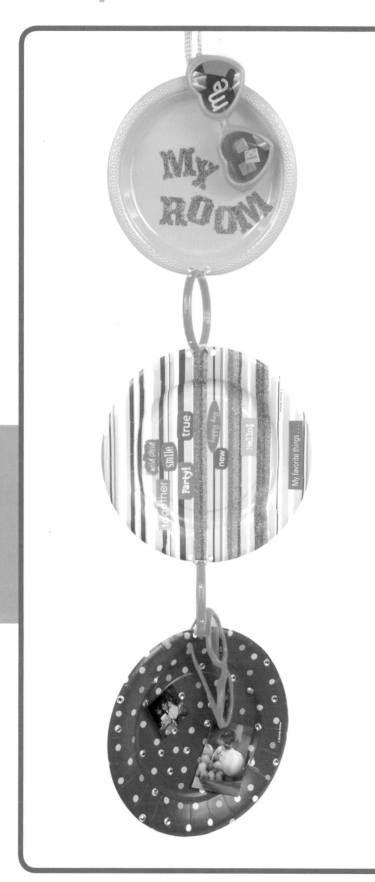

What you need:

- Paper plates
- Cool-temperature glue gun/ glue sticks
- Embellishments
- Office supplies
- Plastic bracelets
- Ribbon

Instructions

1. Decorate plates with office supplies and embellishments.

2. Connect plates by punching 2 holes in the bottom and top of each plate. Using ribbon, tie a bracelet to the plate.

3. Glue lightweight picture frame with favorite picture to bottom of ribbon.

4. Hang over your desk or on the door to your room.

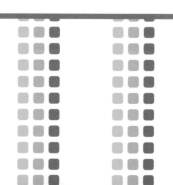

What you need:

- Paper plates
- Cool-temperature glue gun/ glue sticks
- Embellishments
- Office supplies
- Pictures and picture frame
- Ribbon

Instructions

1. Decorate plates with office supplies and embellishments.

2. Connect the plates by adhering the ribbon to the back of the plates. Make a bow at top of ribbon.

3. Glue lightweight picture frame with favorite picture to bottom of ribbon.

4. Hang over your desk or on the door to your room.

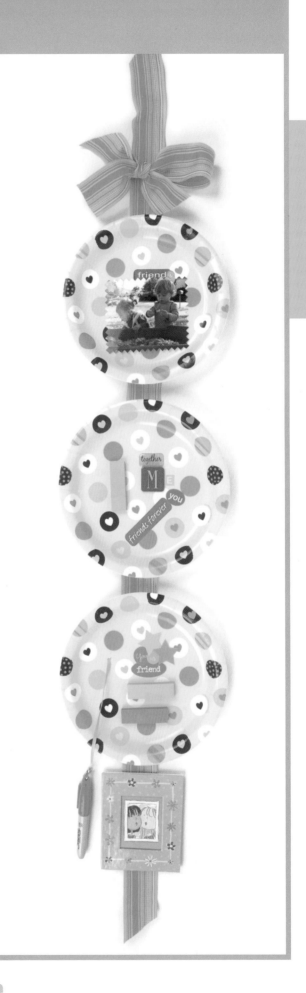

Memo Pocket & Flower Set

What you need:

- 1 large plate
- 1 small plate
- 2 cups
- Cool-temperature glue gun/ glue sticks
- Fresh flowers
- Hole punch
- Memo pads
- Pencil
- Ribbon
- Ruler
- Scissors

Instructions

1. Using pencil and ruler, mark a straight line across center back of small plate. Cut plate in half.

2. Push plate rim "out" to make pocket.

3. Glue pocket to rim of large plate.

4. Punch holes in either side of large plate and attach ribbon.

5. Punch a hole through the plate, and tie a ribbon through hole.

6. Tie a pencil to the end of the ribbon.

7. Tuck memo pads inside pocket.

8. Fill cups with fresh flowers.

9. This is the perfect something special to give to Mom for her desk!

EASY FUN PROJECTS WITH

Jars

Jo Packham

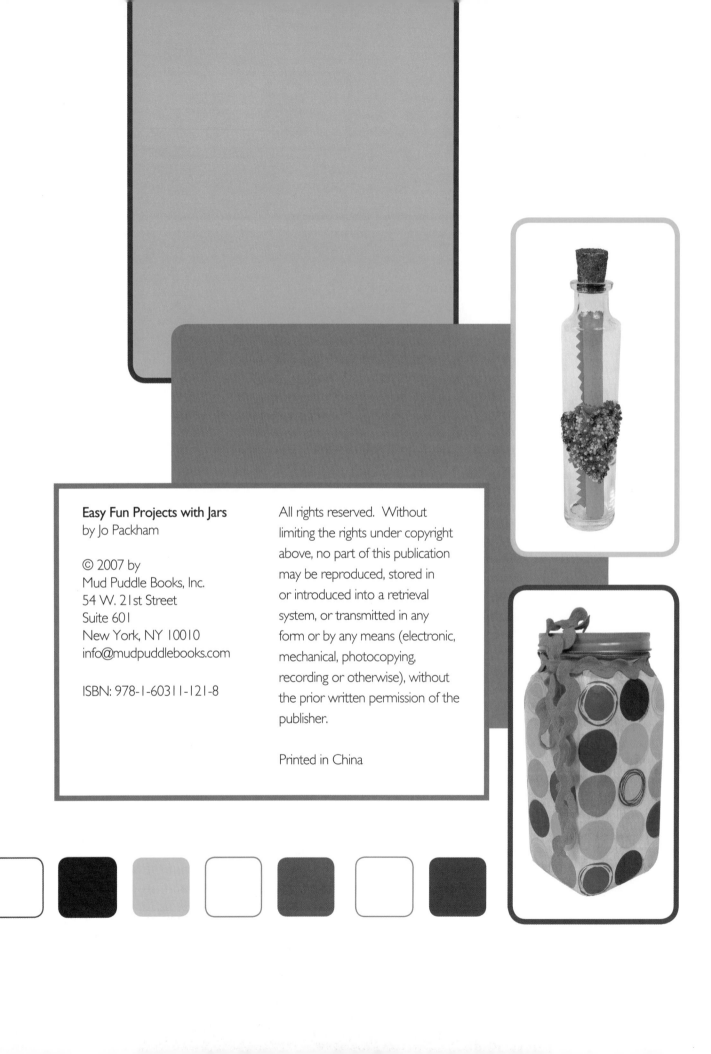

Easy Fun Projects with Jars
by Jo Packham

© 2007 by
Mud Puddle Books, Inc.
54 W. 21st Street
Suite 601
New York, NY 10010
info@mudpuddlebooks.com

ISBN: 978-1-60311-121-8

Printed in China

Table of Contents

Working with bottles and jars that are usually thrown away can be more fun than you ever imagined. They come in so many shapes and sizes, and can be used for hundreds of things. Jars can be glass or plastic, big or small, tall and thin, or short and fat. Some even look like drinking glasses or mugs when the food is gone and the label is off. Bottles and jars can make the perfect "package" for a gift. They can hold anything and everything, and are so very easy for anyone to decorate!

When you are working with bottles and jars, there are two supplies that make all the difference: paint and adhesives. You need to make sure that you are working with the right product for the type of jar you are decorating, as well as for the type of design you are using.

Paint

It is very important that you use the right paint for the job. If you do not, your project will be ruined in a very short period of time. There are five types of paint that you will want to have on hand:

Craft Paint

1 This can be used on the jars or the lids if they are primed first. If not, the paint will scrape off when touched.

Metal Paint

2 This is the right paint for metal lids. It is, however, not water soluble, so you will need to clean it up according to manufacturer's instructions. This paint can also be used on glass and it is fairly long-wearing.

Glass Paint

3 Glass paint: this is the perfect paint for the bottles themselves, however, this paint is very transparent. If you want a design that is opaque, you will need to use oil paint, metal paint, or craft paint and primer.

Rubber Stamp Inks

4 Rubber Stamp Inks: these will be transparent when stamped onto the jars. If you want a more opaque design, you will need to stamp with paint.

Adhesives

Again, it is very important that you use the right product for the job, or you will find that your designs are very temporary.

When adhering anything to your jar, make sure you place one edge of the piece carefully on the jar, then smooth the piece across the jar as you adhere it. If you just stick the piece down on the jar, it will not be smooth.

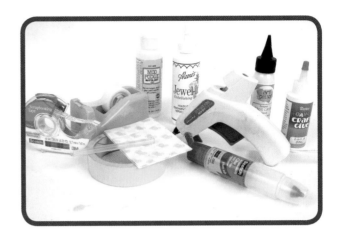

White Glue/ Découpage Glue

1 This can be used to adhere most designs to your jar. The problem with using this glue is that it does not dry very quickly. If you cannot lay your jar down while the glue dries, the pieces may slide off the jar.

Epoxy

2 This glue is needed for permanent, waterproof adhesion, like the glue that is used in water globes. Epoxy is very messy, so be careful and follow the manufacturer's instructions.

Clear Craft Glue

3 This can be used in place of white glue; however, it also does not dry quickly and it cannot be used for découpage.

Adhesive Dots

4 These easy-to-use dots are permanent and adhere to even the smallest of surfaces.

Cool-temperature Glue Gun/Glue Sticks

5 This glue is good when you need quick adhesion; however, it will show if you can see the back of the design through the glass. Be careful when using a glue gun and follow the manufacture's instructions.

Made from Scratch

What you need: (for 1 jar)

- Large jar
- Dry ingredients for favorite recipe
- Double-stick tape
- Favorite photo that is indicative of ingredients
- Hole punch
- Index card or recipe card
- Pinking shears
- Recipe
- Ribbon
- Scrap of fabric

Instructions

1. Measure fabric approximately 2" (5.1cm) larger than lid. Cut with shears. Cut two long ribbon strips.

2. Rim the back side of the photo with 4 strips of double-stick tape, then stick to jar.

3. Gather dry ingredients for favorite recipe, then layer all ingredients in jar.

4. Type or write recipe on index or recipe card.

5. Use ribbon to tie fabric over lid, punch hole in recipe card, and tie onto jar.

Mini Pumpkin Muffins

What you need:

- Non-stick spray coating
- 1⅓ cups (320 ml) all-purpose flour
- ¾ cup (180 ml) buckwheat flour
- ⅓ cup (80 ml) sugar
- 1½ teaspoons (7.5 ml) baking powder
- 1 teaspoon (5 ml) ground cinnamon
- ½ teaspoon (2.5 ml) baking soda
- ½ teaspoon (2.5 ml) salt
- 2 slightly beaten eggs
- 1 cup (240 ml) canned pumpkin
- ½ cup (120 ml) fat-free milk
- 2 tablespoons (30 ml) cooking oil
- ¼ cup (60 ml) orange juice

Optional: Chocolate chips, nuts, raisins, or top with butter cream frosting

Instructions

1. Spray 2 miniature muffin pans with non-stick coating; set pans aside. In a medium bowl combine the all-purpose flour, buckwheat flour, sugar, baking powder, cinnamon, baking soda, and salt. Make a well in the center of flour mixture; set aside.

2. In another bowl, combine the eggs, pumpkin, milk, oil, orange juice, and chocolate chips, raisins, or nuts. Add the egg mixture all at once to the flour mixture. Stir just until moistened (batter should be lumpy).

3. Spoon batter into the prepared muffin cups, dividing the batter evenly. Bake in a 400° F (205° C) oven for 15 to 20 minutes or until the muffins are light brown. Cool in muffin pan on a wire rack for 5 minutes. Remove; serve warm.

Butter Cream Frosting

- ¼ cup (60 ml) melted butter
- Dash of salt
- 2 cups (480 ml) powdered sugar
- 3 tablespoons (45 ml) cream or milk
- 1 teaspoon (5 ml) vanilla

Stir all ingredients together and mix well. Spread over cooled muffins. *Note: You can also add food coloring to make different colors of frosting, or add sprinkles for holiday decorating.*

Vintage Candy Jars

What you need: (for 1 jar)

- Jar
- 2 vintage fabric designs
- Découpage or white glue
- Old-fashioned candy
- Paintbrush

Instructions

1 Cut each fabric design about 2" (5.1cm) larger than rim and lid

2 Cover lid with glue.

3 Smooth one fabric over lid.

4 Spread glue on side of of lid and wrap second fabric around.

5 Let dry, then fill jar with candy.

Button Flower Jars

What you need: (for 1 jar)

- Small jar
- Adhesive dots
- Metal paint
- Paintbrush
- Variety of trims: buttons, paper, ribbon, Ric Rac,* etc

Instructions

1 Paint jar lid and let dry.

2 Glue paper and trims onto jar to make flower designs.

* A narrow zigzag ribbon used as trimming.

Photo Jars

What you need:

- Jars
- Favorite photographs
- Metal paints
- Paintbrush

Instructions

1. Paint lids and let dry.
2. Cut pictures to fit exactly from top to bottom of jar.
3. Place photograph in jar.
4. Use in place of picture frames.

Happy Birthday!

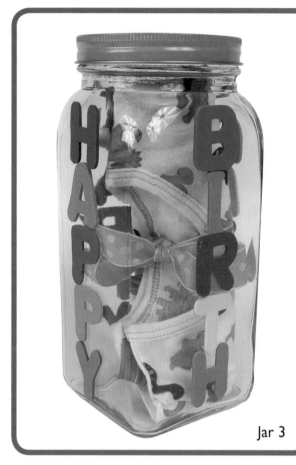

Jar 3

What you need:

- 3 large jars
- Découpage or white glue
- Letter stickers: foam or paper
- Metal paints
- Paintbrush
- Ric Rac or ribbon
- Tissue paper
- Wrapping paper or wrapping tape

Jar 1

Jar 2

Instructions

1. Paint lids and let dry.
2. Découpage tissue onto jar 1. *Note: If tissue is too transparent, découpage a matching second layer.*
3. Let dry.
4. Wrap tape or wrapping paper around the base of jar 2.
5. Stick letters with desired saying to jar 3.
6. Fill jars with gifts such as candy, rolled t-shirts, etc.

Message in a Bottle

What you need:

- Tall, skinny jar
- Colored paper
- Cork or lid
- Glitter
- Paintbrush
- Ribbon
- White glue
- Sticker (optional)

Instructions

1 Paint cork or lid with glue and cover with glitter.

2 Adhere sticker or make your own embellishment to stick on jar front.

3 Write a letter, roll it up, tie with ribbon, and put in bottle.

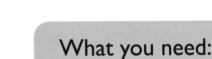

What you need:

- Jar
- Colored paper
- Double-stick tape
- Glitter
- Glitter alphabet stickers
- Paintbrush
- White glue

Wish Jars

Instructions

1 Paint lid with glue and cover with glitter.

2 Put a strip of double-stick tape around jar, then cover with glitter.

3 Add name or initials in glitter stickers.

4 Write wishes on strips of paper and fill jar.

Home Movies

What you need:

- 4-pack of soda pop in cardboard carton
- Adhesive dots
- Candy
- Double-stick tape
- Embellishment
- Hole punch
  Popcorn kernels
- Ribbon
  Scissors
  Variety of heavy paper
- Movie rental card (optional)

Instructions

1. Cut heavy paper to cover sides of carton. Adhere with double-stick tape.

2. Cut rectangles to wrap around middle of bottles. Adhere with double-stick tape.

3. Cut circles, squares, and rectangles from papers. Decorate carton and bottles.

4. Drink the soda pop from 2 bottles, then wash thoroughly. Let dry. Fill one bottle with popcorn and one with candy.

5. Place embellishment on top of one bottle and stick in place with adhesive.

6. Make tag from paper, punch a hole, and tie onto bottle with ribbon.

   Optional: Hang free movie rental cards from bottles.

Water Globes

Instructions

1. Paint jar lids. Let dry.

2. Sand the inside of the lid until the metal is scratched.

3. Following manufacturer's instructions, use clear-drying epoxy to adhere the miniature to the inside of the lid. Let epoxy dry.

4. Fill the jar almost to the top with distilled water. Add glitter and a dash of glycerin to keep the glitter from falling too quickly. *Note: if you add too much glitter it will stick to the bottom of the jar.*

5. Screw the lid on tightly, being careful not to spill the water or dislodge the miniature.

What you need: (for 1 jar)

- Baby food jar with tight-fitting lids
- Course sandpaper
- Distilled water
- Epoxy glue
- Glitter
- Glycerin (available at the pharmacy)
- Metal paint
- Miniatures, ceramic figurines, or plastic toys (do not use metal—they rust)
- Paintbrush

More Gifts for You

What you need: (for 1 box)

- Baby food jar
  Confetti
- Gift box & ribbon
- Large adhesive dots
- Metal paint
- Paintbrush

Instructions

1. Paint lid. Let dry.

2. Fill jar with confetti and screw on lid.

3. Place present inside gift box and tie bow. Adhere bottle to center of bow with adhesive dots.

Wish Upon Star

What you need:

- Tall, skinny jar
- Double-stick tape
- Metal paint
- Paintbrush
- Printed saying
- Star confetti

Instructions

1. Paint lid. Let dry.

2. Print sentiment either by hand or with a computer.

3. Tape sentiment to bottle.

4. Fill with stars.

I Wish I May, I Wish I Might

Votive Candles

What you need:
- Baby food jars
- Adhesive rhinestones
- Glass paints
- Paintbrush
- Tea lights

Instructions

1. Paint outside of jars. Let dry.
2. Add rhinestones as desired.
3. Add tea lights.

Bubble Bottles

What you need:

- Soda pop bottles with screw-on lids
- Alphabet stickers
- Bubble mixture
- Bubble blowers
- Epoxy
- Metal Paints
- Paintbrush

Instructions

1 Paint lids. Let dry.

2 Following one of the sets of bubble instructions, make bubble mixture and fill bottles.

3 Epoxy bubble blowers to bottle lids following manufacturer's instructions

4 Use stickers to write guests' names on the bottles.

All-Purpose Bubble Solution

What you need:

- 7–10 parts water
- 1 part dish detergent
- Glycerin (available at the pharmacy)

Instructions

1 Combine water, detergent, and 1–2 tablespoons (15-30 ml) of glycerin.

Outdoor Thick Bubble Solution

This is a thick, goopy solution that forms bubbles strong enough to withstand a small puff of air. You can blow bubbles inside of bubbles with this mixture, and you don't need a straw. Just make a bubble and blow!

What you need:

- 2-½–3 parts water
- 1 part dish detergent
- Glycerin (available at the pharmacy)

Instructions

1 Combine water, detergent, and 1–2 tablespoons (15-30 ml) of glycerin.

Bouncy Bubble Solution

What you need:

- 2 packages unflavored gelatin
- 4 cups (.95 liter) hot water (just boiled)
- 3–5 tablespoons (45-75 ml) glycerin (available at the pharmacy)
- 3 tablespoons (45 ml) dish detergent

Instructions

1 Dissolve the gelatin in hot water. Add glycerin and dish detergent. This mixture will gel, so you'll need to reheat it whenever you use it.

Mosaic Jars

What you need: (for 1 jar)

- Jar with even square sides or round with no writing in the glass
- Adhesive dots or double-stick tape
- Scissors
- Tape measure
- Variety of paper cut into squares
- Gel mosaics found in craft and hobby stores (optional)

Instructions

1 Measure width of jar and cut squares of paper so that they will fit around jar. Example: if the jar has a 7" (17.8 cm) flat side, then you would make three 2" (5.1 cm) squares so that you will have space between them, or six 1" (2.5 cm) squares leaving one inch space to divide between the squares.

2 Put adhesive dot on the back of each paper square and adhere to jar.

18

Hanging Plant

What you need:
- Jar with metal screwband portion of lid
- Live plant
- Metal paint
- Paintbrush
- Ribbon

Instructions

1 Paint lid

2 Place plant in jar.

3 Tie ribbon through three sides of lid and up around jar.

4 Tie ribbons in large knot at top and hang plant

Pamper Yourself

Instructions

1. Purchase or make gels and shampoos following the instructions listed, then pour into bottles.

2. Decorate with stickers and ribbons as desired.

What you need: (for 1 jar)

- Bottle
- Adhesive dots or double-stick tape
- Bubble bath, gel, and conditioner
- Embellishments
- Scissors

Grapefruit Bubble Bath

What you need:

- ½ cup (120 ml) unscented shampoo (baby shampoo is best)
- ½ cup (120 ml) glycerin (available at the pharmacy)
- ½ teaspoon (2.5 ml) table salt
- ¾ cup (180 ml) water
- 2 drops red, orange, or light green food coloring
- 15 drops grapefruit oil

Grapefruit Shower Gel

What you need:

Same recipe as bubble bath with these exceptions:

- ¾ teaspoon (3.75 ml) table salt
- 1 drop food coloring
- Add 1 teaspoon (5 ml) powdered loofah (optional)

Instructions (for all gels)

1. Combine shampoo, glycerin, and water in a bowl. Stir gently until well mixed.

2. Add salt, and stir until mixture thickens. Add fragrance oil and food coloring, then pour mixture into decorative bottle or jar.

Grapefruit Hair Conditioner

What you need:

- ½ cup (120 ml) cholesterol-type conditioner (available at beauty supply shops and drugstores)
- ¾ cup (180 ml) water
- 15 drops grapefruit oil
- 1 drop red orange coloring

Note: For oily hair, add one tablespoon (15 ml) aloe vera gel to your conditioner. It will help moisturize without excess oil. For dry hair, add one tablespoon (15 ml) of corn oil to your conditioner.

Halloween Monsters

What you need:

- Baby food or round jars with big lids
- Adhesive dots
- Embellishments
- Halloween candy
- Metal paints
- Paintbrush

Instructions

1 Paint lids and jars. Let dry.

2 Make faces using markers and embellishments. Affix with adhesive dots.

3 Fill jars with candy.

Christmas Candy Jars

What you need:

- Jars
- Cool-temperature glue gun/ glue sticks
- Double-stick tape
- Embellishments: cork, pipe cleaner, Ric Rac, star, stickers, tags
- Metal paints
- Paintbrush

Instructions

1. Paint jar lids and accents on bottles. Let dry.

2. Decorate bottles anyway you like.

3. Fill with candy, add gift tag, and give away!

Note: To make tree, bend pipe cleaner into tree shape, stick trunk into cork, glue cork to lid.

Memo Board

What you need:

- Small baby food jars
- Adhesive letters
- Baking pan
- Cool-temperature glue gun/ glue sticks or epoxy
- Metal paints
- Paintbrush
- Picture hanger
- Strong magnets

Instructions

1. Paint lids. Let dry.
2. Glue one magnet to the bottom of each jar and picture hanger to back of baking pan.
3. Place initial of item to be placed in jar on lid. For example: paperclips = P.
4. Place bottles on baking pan. Hang on wall.

Note: Popsicles are erasers attached with glue dots.

What you need:

- Variety of bottles
- Découpage or white glue
- Embellishments: adhesive letters, rhinestones, ribbon, pen topper such as a flower or feather
- Metal paints
- Pen
- Ribbon
- Sand
- Small flat brush

Desk Set

Instructions

1. Paint lid of small bottle. Let dry.
2. Paint bottles with tiny square strokes and dots. Let dry.
3. Add rhinestones, letters, and ribbons as desired.
4. Hold pen and pen topper to be wrapped together. Starting at the top, wrap ribbon around both pen and flower stem or feather. Glue end of ribbon by the point of the pen.
5. Fill small jar with sand to make a paperweight.

Jewerly Jars

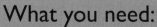

What you need:

- Shallow jars
- Embellishments or jewelry pieces
- Cool-temperature glue gun/ glue stick
- Metal paints
- Paintbrush

Instructions

1. Paint lids. Let dry.
2. Adhere jewelry pieces or other embellishments to lid.

Vases

What you need:

- Soda pop bottles
- Embellishments: foam stickers, ribbons, or any waterproof item of your choice

Instructions

1. Decorate soda bottles as desired with chosen embellishments.

World Globe Paperweight

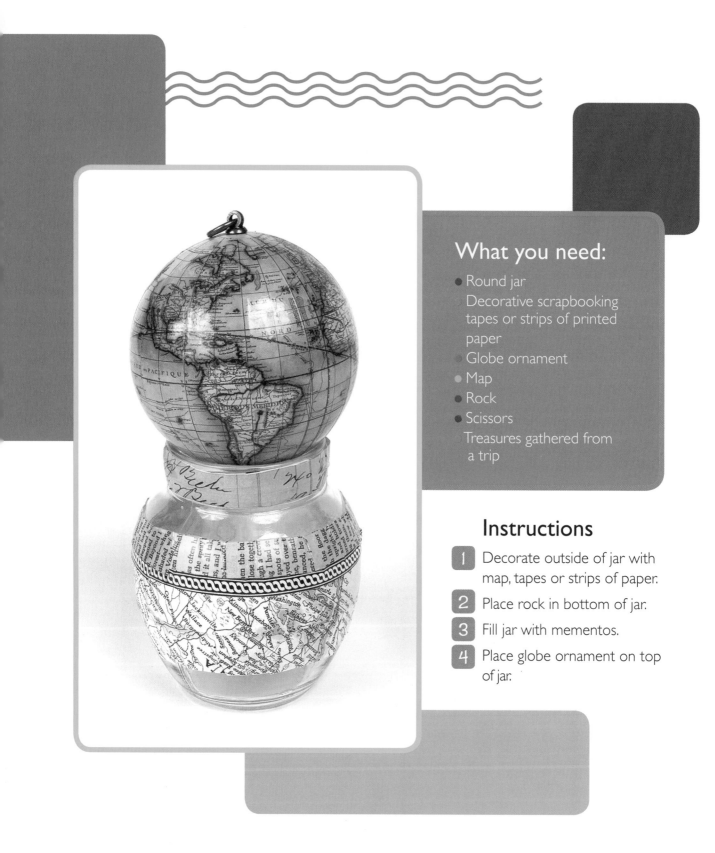

What you need:

- Round jar
  Decorative scrapbooking tapes or strips of printed paper
- Globe ornament
- Map
- Rock
- Scissors
  Treasures gathered from a trip

Instructions

1 Decorate outside of jar with map, tapes or strips of paper.

2 Place rock in bottom of jar.

3 Fill jar with mementos.

4 Place globe ornament on top of jar.

Compass Jar

What you need:

- Round jar
- Black marker
- Double-stick tape
- Gold and tan cardstock
- Hole punch
- Ribbon
- Scrapbook grommet

Instructions

1. Cut circle the size of lid from tan cardstock.

2. Draw compass pattern onto tan cardstock circle.

3. Cut arrow from gold cardstock, punch hole in center, and connect arrow to compass with grommet. Adhere to jar.

4. Wrap and adhere ribbon around lip of lid.

Butterfly Jar

What you need:

- Tall, glass jar
- Butterflies (can be purchased at the craft or floral supply store)
- Metal paint
- Paintbrush
- Small tree branch
- Thin wire

Instructions

1. Paint lid. Let dry.
2. Wire butterflies to branch and place inside jar.

What you need:
- Jars
- Grass, moss, rocks
- Metal paint
- Paintbrush
- Plastic bugs, frogs, snakes, and spiders

Instructions

1 Paint lids. Let dry.

2 Put grass, moss, and rocks in bottom of jars.

3 Arrange bugs, frogs, snakes, and spiders in the grass and rocks.